LEADING
the DEAL

LEADING the DEAL

THE SECRET TO SUCCESSFUL ACQUISITION AND INTEGRATION

Thras Moraitis and Carlos Keener

urbanepublications.com

First published in Great Britain in 2018 by Urbane Publications Ltd
Suite 3, Brown Europe House, 33/34 Gleaming Wood Drive, Chatham, Kent ME5 8RZ
Copyright © Thras Moraitis and Carlos Keener, 2019

The moral right of Thras Moraitis and Carlos Keener to be identified as the authors
of this work has been asserted in accordance with the Copyright, Designs and
Patents Act of 1988.

A CIP catalogue record for this book is available from the British Library.

ISBN 978-1-912666-07-2
MOBI 978-1-912666-08-9

Design and Typeset by Julie Martin
Cover by Julie Martin

Printed and bound by 4edge UK

Urbane
BUSINESS

urbanepublications.com

CONTENTS

ACKNOWLEDGEMENTS   9

FOREWORD   15

Chapter 1:
BEGIN WITH THE END IN MIND   27

Chapter 2:
BUSINESS IS WAR... BUT WHAT ABOUT THE PEACE?   61

Chapter 3:
CHANGE IS EXPECTED – DON'T DISAPPOINT   90

Chapter 4:
BUILD AND SUSTAIN MOMENTUM   118

Chapter 5:
OPPORTUNITY AND RISK: THE GEMINI TWINS OF INTEGRATION   144

Chapter 6:
BUILD POWERFUL TEAMS AND MAKE THEM ACCOUNTABLE   167

Chapter 7:
COMMUNICATE, COMMUNICATE, LISTEN, COMMUNICATE   188

Chapter 8:
STAY THE COURSE THROUGH MEASUREMENT   206

Chapter 9:
WHEN ALL IS SAID AND DONE   225

INDEX   235

ACKNOWLEDGEMENTS

THRAS MORAITIS

Experience is about opportunity and success is about collaboration.

I have been fortunate many times in my life to be given opportunities that, perhaps, I was not deserving of at the time. These expressions of generosity and blind trust were usually the ones which led to my most cherished experiences, providing the most intense learning and greatest stretch.

Having the opportunity to lead the integration of MIM into Xstrata in 2003, and Falconbridge into Xstrata in 2006 – a $20bn acquisition which created a company with some 100 operations across 20 countries – were once-in-a-lifetime opportunities. Many of the learnings distilled into this short book stem from transactions like these. I would like to thank my colleagues Mick Davis and Trevor Reid, then CEO and CFO of Xstrata Plc respectively, for taking the chance on a once young and eager man and for entrusting me with what turned out to be two seminal transactions in Xstrata's remarkable journey. Their conviction and support through these and other complex transactions created fertile conditions for learning, but also, I believe, success. It was, in fact, Mick's rare understanding of the importance of post-acquisition integration as an integral part of the M&A journey from the very start, that ensured Xstrata's success in its acquisition of some 30 companies over the period of a decade and enabled us to create a group-wide integration core competence – a clear source of advantage for serial acquirers. It is precisely this form of leadership and its role in the M&A process that this book is aimed at highlighting.

In reality, it was the dedication of many colleagues at Xstrata who, under very trying conditions, made the various transactions we embarked on a success. To them, I owe a debt of gratitude not only for their commitment and skill, but also for challenging me at every step of the way, thereby ensuring our approach was continuously relevant and evolving.

Carlos Keener, my co-author, has walked alongside the Xstrata and X2 Resources team for numerous years, bringing his wise counsel and experience to our post-deal integration approach, helping us capture the essence and details into an interactive knowledge-base which underpinned our core competence. Carlos, thank you for the spirit of collaboration which characterised the writing of this book, itself a process which has contributed much to my learning.

My thanks go to Matthew Smith at Urbane for understanding

the desired tone and audience of this book from its genesis and for guiding us through the process of transforming a few scraps of paper into a published book.

Finally, I would like to thank my unfailingly patient family – my extraordinary wife and soulmate, Soula, who has unconditionally and unquestioningly supported me as I lurch from one project to another, often hare-brained, sometimes worthwhile; and my children Dino and Irene, who continually delight me with their undying support and humour my grumbling about one deadline or another. I am proud and blessed to have a family so loving, so accomplished and so complete. You are every fibre of my being.

CARLOS KEENER

This book represents a culmination of learning and experience from myself and my team, having led, supported or simply witnessed over 100 acquisitions and integrations over more than two decades. We've done so as corporate business leaders, management consultants, and – possibly most importantly – as employee foot soldiers being on the receiving end of the good, the bad, and the ugly of acquiring, being acquired and being integrated. We've seen – first-hand – acquiring CEOs promising to retain and value their culture and heritage…as the acquired company logo literally came crashing down off the outside walls without a trace of sympathy or even irony. We've seen too many 'joint CEO' arrangements, all with the best of intentions…and seen them lose credibility within days as they chaotically, painfully unravel within months. We've seen senior Corporate IT Directors fighting to ensure that their own homegrown finance system be selected as the joint way forward, despite renouncing the beast only weeks before, staking (and of course on one side, losing) their entire future careers on 'winning the contest against the other guy'. We've heard everything from "why bother measuring success, my boss doesn't care anymore so why should I?" to "we don't need help delivering any deal benefits, they'll take care of themselves; we only want help with integration" to "the best way to help employees through this integration is to tell them nothing at all until it's all finished."

But we've also seen things that I can only describe as inspirational, things that taught me what's truly important in this field. CEOs who stood up in front of their newly-acquired employees – from the factory floor up – and told them in detail why the deal was done, what they had that his own team didn't, what it had cost, how much they had borrowed, and what exactly they were hoping to do together to make sure everyone worked in a stronger, better place within 12 months. I've seen managers at all levels put their heart and soul into building a better future for their teams and businesses, alongside a day job that already took up every waking hour of their day. I've seen executives create a new combined business from the ground up with passion, commitment and professionalism – all the while openly, constructively recognising that the future organisation they were creating wasn't going to be the right place for them. And we've heard CEOs ask the right questions: "How do I make sure my senior team understands this deal and are genuinely committed to making it work; or if they aren't, feel able to tell me to kill it?", "Are we truly the best owners of this business?", "Forget the numbers and the process for a moment – what does the future look and feel like as a single business, and why should our customers and employees care?"

This experience – and this book – would not have been possible without my Partners, our team, our clients, and the much broader group of M&A and integration professionals within our network, all of whom have, in one way or another, consciously or not, informed and contributed to this book. Every story, lesson, and piece of advice you will read here has come from them. They – in addition to making the last 18 years of my time with BTD both fulfilling and fun – are the real authors of this book. Too numerous to mention by name (but Thras is at the top of this list!), I'd like to take this opportunity to express my deep gratitude to them all, and offer every one of them at least a drink when we're next together.

Thras and I would also like to give a special note of thanks to Peter Koczerzat, who more than anyone made this book a reality through his very considerable efforts and determination putting our unstructured thoughts, random musings, receding experiences, and occasional disagreements, into words on a page. We wish Peter the best in his career and look forward to his undoubted future successes.

And finally, to my wife Patricia, and sons Andrew and Patrick; without their unwavering love, encouragement and support over the years this book, and so much else besides, would never have been within my ambition, let alone reach. While (as every father should) I wish you even greater success than I have enjoyed in my career, I'd be hard pressed to imagine you being able to find a stronger and happier family than the one I am fortunate enough to enjoy.

FOREWORD

We have all heard of high profile M&A failures – HP-Compaq, Daimler-Chrysler, AOL-Time Warner – the list seems endless.[1] In their recent assessment of 2,500 transactions, the consulting firm LEK calculates that 60% fail to create shareholder value. Other research argues that failure rates are even higher.[2]

Naturally, a high proportion of these failures can be ascribed to ill-conceived strategic rationales or fatal culture clashes. The rest are down to poor integration execution.

The even higher failure rate of M&A a couple of decades ago resulted from an environment almost devoid of formalised management science reflecting the best practice of M&A and integration. This void encouraged academics, consultants and managers to contribute to the body of knowledge of managing integration. By the early 1990s, integration became more of a science – consulting firms offered bespoke integration

---

1: (Lewis and McKone, 2016) https://hbr.org/2016/05/so-many-ma-deals-fail-because-companies-overlook-this-simple-strategy

2: Koi-Akrofi, Godfred. (2016). Mergers and Acquisitions failure rates and perspectives on why they fail. International Journal of Innovation and Applied Studies. 17. 150-158.

services to help improve their clients' tools and processes, more academic attention led to swathes of books on the process of post-merger integration, and managers began to see integration as a change management exercise.

At the same time, globalisation and the disruption of one industry after another by new technologies and business models have increased the prominence of M&A as a strategy execution tool. The number of transactions continue to increase year after year.

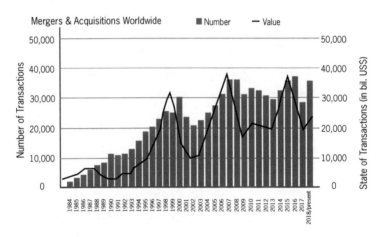

Reference: (imaa, 2019)[3]

Despite these trends, CEOs remain rightly anxious about embarking on an M&A process, especially post-deal integration. Companies pour money into the process, making

3: Ref: https://imaa-institute.org/mergers-and-acquisitions-statistics/

extensive use of consultants, change theory and resources. Even smaller serial acquirers have well-established integration checklists, playbooks and tools to make sure nothing is left to chance. Further, CEOs often ensure seasoned integration managers are on hand to guide and monitor integration initiatives.

The market is replete with books and approaches laying out the need for, and providing guidance on, a systematic approach to M&A and integration that methodically covers all the bases, aiming to manage risk, and providing comprehensive checklists for every step of the journey. The better ones also consider the famous 'softer' aspects we also know to be critical: culture, communications, employee engagement and others. These frameworks have begun to coalesce around a recognisable set of processes, tools, internal teams and conventional wisdoms.

This step change in the use of frameworks and tools and in the investment of time, effort and resources has not yet translated into universal success. In fact, many companies are still getting it wrong – regularly. At the very least, success – delivering the objectives of the transaction and improving shareholder value – is patchy. With the exception of some prominent acquirers or lucky one-off transactions, M&A remains a risky enterprise for companies and their executive teams.

Even more tantalising is the observation that some organisations do appear to get it right, consistently. Firms such as CISCO, Oracle, Pfizer, P&G, WPP, Xstrata and others have historically increased share price through successful acquisition and integration. Similarly, GE, Microsoft, IBM and Google are often seen as consistent M&A winners but occasionally find themselves in the news for M&A disappointments. A superficial investigation leads to no firm correlation: size, sector, deal type and methodology don't necessarily guarantee success.

CISCO for example seems universally recognised for their acquisitions, largely because 'practice makes (mostly) perfect'. But even CISCO has struggled with integration over the last 10 years.[4]

So what's going on?

This book *does not* attempt to add to or improve upon the plethora of processes, toolboxes, checklists or templates aimed at delivering a slick post-transaction process.

What we are aiming to do is to highlight the 'missing ingredients' – the secret sauce, if you like – essential to *accompany* the now well-established approaches in order to improve the chances of success. It goes to the *psychology* of

---

4: (Cheng, 2011) Digitalhttps://arstechnica.com/gadgets/2011/04/two-years-after-buying-pure-digital-cisco-ditches-the-flip/

successful post-transaction processes – less easily defined topics of self-confidence, balance of energy, integrity of communication, the power of leadership and the like.

This book covers an entirely different set of success factors for integration than those traditionally addressed: the attitudes, behaviours and actions of the senior executives leading the acquiring business. The 'inconvenient truth' is that these executive leadership behaviours directly determine the success – or failure – of a business's M&A strategy, often without these same leaders consciously understanding the impact they're having, good or bad. Like it or not, these behaviours can largely inform, if not pre-determine, M&A success even before any specific deal is on the table. If a business has consistently failed at M&A in the past, and if it is believed that failure is due to systemic issues within the business culture, the chances are the business will fail with future projects.

That's not to say that 'nothing can be done', or that your M&A destiny is unchangeable. Like any culture or set of behaviours, patience, incentives, leading by example and refining the priorities and actions of those at the top can and does make a huge difference. With focus and effort, good integration leadership can be learned. This book, based on over 50 years of combined author experience and a review of over 150 companies completing hundreds of deals, is designed to help you do just that.

This book is not a comprehensive 'soup-to-nuts' guide on designing and executing an M&A strategy. Rather, it is targeted at busy CEOs, CFOs and other members of the executive committee who are about to embark on an M&A adventure, and who ultimately bear the responsibility for the success or failure of the transaction. In this book we aim to provide you with a set of prompts – and some suggestions – to help you ensure your M&A strategy includes the key ingredients for success at each point in the process. It will also prove the perfect starting point for aspiring business leaders, providing valuable insights into psychology, culture and leadership behaviours that play such a critical role in the M&A process.

We want to guide you in the questions you should be asking your M&A and integration teams to ensure the frameworks are supplemented with the less-well documented success factors fundamental to the leadership of the process: setting the correct tone at the outset, sustaining the momentum, creating accountability, adopting the right pace for success, and so on.

Throughout this book, you will note some consistent themes which underpin our philosophical perspective on what distinguishes successful integrations:

- *Accountability*: Ensuring clear accountability for each task and the overall delivery of the integration process throughout;

- *Balancing Opportunity and Risk:* The key balancing act is delivering the promise of the deal, while not breaking the business;

• *Building and Sustaining Momentum:* Momentum is the life-blood of a successful integration. If the aircraft stalls, it will fall from the sky;

• *Visible Leadership:* Senior executives cannot run from the complexity of integration – antithetically, they need to raise their profiles significantly;

• *Focusing on the 'me' issues:* Without managing the anxieties of individuals and groups, the process cannot move forward as required;

• *Communicating Bidirectionally:* Shout from the rooftops and listen on the shop floor; and

• *Measuring what is to be Managed:* Use metrics to monitor progress, pre-empt derailments and sustain momentum.

Above all, *Leadership* is predictably the key differentiating factor between success and failure. Don't skimp on this and understand specifically what it means for your M&A efforts.

The book is laid out to reflect these key themes, all of which apply across the entire M&A process.

In *Chapter 1* we elaborate on some of the principles outlined here, underlining the need to start integration planning early and allocating the best resources to the process.

Chapter 2 discusses the impact of your reputation – especially as an acquirer – on setting the tone for the post-acquisition process.

The importance of getting a quick start and building momentum is examined in *Chapter 3*. Both your and your target's organisations are expecting change – giving you a licence to bring about a new combined business. Failure to take this opportunity quickly results in the organisation re-ossifying and hence becoming difficult to change.

Building and sustaining the momentum of the launch is a difficult task, especially in the face of inevitable resistance. Until the central question "what does this mean for me?" is satisfactorily addressed – for your own top team and customers as well as employees – it's hard to build up a full head of steam. We discuss managing resistance and creating the conditions for a speedy integration process in *Chapter 4*.

Integration processes represent a fine and complex balancing act between opportunity, risk, speed and quality; a place where the 'perfect' is regularly the enemy of the 'good enough for now'. Often, we get caught up in potential positive outcomes and downplay the risks that can derail the transaction. *Chapter 5* highlights the need for detailed planning of all these factors to ensure quick and appropriate responses to the inevitable surprises that will come your way.

Organisations do not comprise a single individual or even a collection of individuals. It is successful, accountable teams which drive the important changes and upon which success is built. In *Chapter 6* we explore the importance of building your new teams around the real issues they will have to tackle as the combined organisation seeks to meet the promise of the transaction.

All executives know that good communication is an everyday requirement. An integration process, however, raises the bar significantly. The heightened anxieties and fertile rumour mill create a highly febrile environment in which logic is not always prevalent. Only through determined and well-planned, bi-directional communication can you ensure that your narrative prevails. We discuss this in *Chapter 7*.

Chapter 8 discusses the role and uses of measurement in the specific context of integration processes. In the world of information systems and big data, organisations are inundated with metrics aimed at understanding every aspect of the business and how it is performing. We examine how these metrics are applied in an integration process, and how they are selected and used to drive insight, commitment and success. A concluding Chapter 9 suggests next steps and encourages the sharing of your M&A experiences.

In summary, integration is about not disrupting operations, rapidly getting the organisation to quickly settle into the desired state, preparing the organisation to extract the value promised in the transaction and setting it up for the next major strategic move as quickly as possible.

We hope you will find this book useful as you contemplate your M&A strategy, embark on a transaction and, hopefully, find yourself in a post-transaction integration process. It's meant to prompt you to ask the key questions at important junctures – the type of questions you won't necessarily find in the myriad frameworks, process maps and checklists that now exist as part of the integration tradecraft.

We are eager to hear from you too. What topics have we not covered, what are your personal experiences, and what has made the difference in integrations in which you have been involved? We'd love to hear your comments at **leadingthedeal@btd.consulting** or at our LinkedIn[5] discussion group <u>Leading the Deal</u>.

5: LinkedIn group: https://www.linkedin.com/groups/8735603/

Chapter 1:
BEGIN WITH THE END IN MIND

"Good business leaders create a vision, articulate the vision, passionately own the vision, and relentlessly drive it to completion."
JACK WELCH

"Great things in business are never done by one person. They're done by a team of people."
STEVE JOBS

"This deal is going to transform his business. Three months after closing Quintado's acquisition of Lidare, with Christmas around the corner, the 100-day plan is largely delivered, on time and on budget. New organisation structures are agreed, people have moved into their new departments, the new branding and signage is all in place, and email addresses are all aligned. Six months into his new role as MD, Paul knew it was time for a well-earned break.

But Paul was anything but relaxed. His story to the market and his board might be 'mission accomplished', but he knew just how hard it had been to get this far, and he suspected worse was to come. Only last week he'd been told that the two 'oldco' sales teams were in open warfare, arguing minutiae over how to manage joint customers; costs to integrate their ERP systems were far higher than he'd been promised last spring; and confusion around the IT product roadmap was growing, not reducing. To top off his Monday morning, his own Finance Director James – the very person who'd brought the deal to the table – resigned, simply stating that he'd 'had enough' and couldn't buy into where he felt Paul was taking the new company. Paul knew this process might be hard for the target company's employees, but his own team? Weren't they all on board from the start?

Thinking back, Paul was certain that integration planning and execution had progressed smoothly, all in line with their well-used integration playbook and without any major problems along the way…and yet everything he and his deal team had put in place – everything he'd promised the board in the run up to the deal – seemed to be unravelling. A quick, straightforward integration based on similar strategies and a close cultural fit; that was the mantra that had carried them through the hard times before the fantastic (and fantastically expensive) Day One event at the casino by the lake. But afterwards, despite hours of 'alignment workshops' and thousands more spent on 'change and engagement' activities, people around the office could be heard talking openly about how 'they' simply weren't interested in making things easier for 'us'. Customers were beginning to complain about helpdesk service problems, and the staff layoffs *scheduled for February now looked like they would need to take place in June; so much for the 'quick wins' he'd promised investors. As for the broader acquisition business case, Paul knew deep down that it was becoming more fiction than fact with every passing week, but couldn't face that conversation with his board before the holiday break. He needed more – and better – information about what they had just bought, where the problems were and how they should move forward, otherwise this might be the shortest MD role in his career.*

Most frustrating of all: Paul had to admit to himself that most of what was coming out of the woodwork was spotted, even discussed if only briefly, well before the deal was completed. What were they – OK, we – thinking?"

Everyone knows that what you do with the new acquisition after deal completion is at least as important as the thinking and work you put into doing the deal itself. People also know that successful acquirers take integration seriously, planning it early, assigning dedicated resources, and managing the effort as rigorously as any other major change programme.

While important, resources and planning will never get you fully over the line. The vision, culture, structure and leadership provide the remaining pieces of the puzzle. The most perfectly executed integration process cannot compensate for deficiencies in these areas.

This opening chapter deals with the two most important

aspects of Integration Leadership: *establishing and maintaining the right environment for the integration*, and linked to this, *getting the right people involved*. Much of what we discuss here relates equally to the pre-close activities as well as the integration itself. Pre-close and post-close activities are better seen as two sides of the same coin, taking place in parallel, each supporting the other. Neither process is able to succeed without the other.

M&A can sometimes feel like a testosterone-fuelled competitive race to the finish, one in which a 'deal done' is considered the ultimate success, and certainly more prestigious and exciting than 'benefits delivered'. If started early and done properly, your integration planning can be (to steal a phrase from George Washington) the 'saucer that cools the tea before it is drunk': it ensures that life post-close is being fully and meticulously considered and used to inform opinions on the long-term viability of the deal. In contrast to the stereotypical and sometimes unproductive environment in which deals are assessed and concluded, successful M&A processes are a collaborative team effort. One in which – while uncertainty abounds – open communication is encouraged, mistakes are positively acknowledged and corrected and unorthodox perspectives are welcomed. In these processes, pressure is not applied to rush the deal, but to do the right deal and do it well. Success is openly measured and judged against the delivery of deal benefits, not just the completing the deal itself. In these exemplary transactions, the M&A and integration teams work together from the start, delivering the right deals in the right way.

Why should I waste precious resources on integration when I don't even know if the deal will go through?

For many, consideration and planning for integration often kicks-off once a merger or acquisition is in the final stages of negotiation and looking likely to complete. In some companies, this work only begins once the transaction has closed. After all, a good due diligence process ensures we understand the business we're looking to buy, defines the expected synergies, validates the strategic rationale, and confirms that the target carries no hidden skeletons or baggage that might disrupt plans post-close. Supported by this work, deal benefits are baked into the budget and objectives, communicated throughout the company and confidently declared to all stakeholders. With the deal complete, the due diligence and M&A teams can (and typically do) wash their hands of the process, sit back and watch the synergies and benefits flow through the company, confident in the knowledge that they have effectively passed responsibility for the new business to the integration and management teams... or can they?

Theory often diverges from reality; like losing weight, the

principles are easy until life's other priorities get in the way. The due diligence process described above can effectively identify the potential synergies if two companies are brought together but it overlooks their compatibility. Where value is driven by fundamentally different operating models and cultures, the idyllic scenario in which they come together in harmony is often farfetched.

Experienced acquirers know that integration should be planned long before the deal itself has closed, even at the risk of 'wasting' time and energy on a plan that may never be executed. In fact, they go further in recognising that integration is not simply a task to be executed once the transaction is nearing completion. Instead, integration design and planning should *inform* the transaction itself – initial target assessment, due diligence, valuation, deal negotiations. In fact your growing knowledge of how integration will play out should ultimately determine whether the deal is worth doing at all. After all, if integration – and all other post-close activities required to deliver the deal benefits – is shown to be too difficult to achieve or too costly to support the business case, then the deal itself should not be pursued, or at least reconsidered under different terms.

Those leading the deal team – or their superiors, if necessary – must ensure that integration (including any other post-close initiatives) is being considered *at every step of the M&A process,* asking themselves and each other the following: If we were to acquire this business:

- Can the businesses fit together, and if so, what would integration look like? What other 'operating model' options (such as partial integration) might be worth considering to maximise deal benefits?

- Which of these operating models would best support the long-term strategy of the new, combined business?

- What challenges would be faced in achieving each of the integration options? How much pressure and risk would integration impose on the ongoing business?

- What are the dependencies impacting your integration strategy? Does success hinge on any one assumption?

By starting integration design early, astute executive teams assess the extent and complexity of the task and the areas in which value could be unlocked or destroyed – the *real* determination of synergies, not one cobbled together by bankers or accountants with insufficient information and often misaligned incentives. The smartest CEOs are those who pull the plug on a transaction because the integration is too complex, regardless of the theoretical upside promised by their deal teams.

Putting Integration Due Diligence into Practice

Cisco's acquisition strategy through the 1990s revolved around employee retention and integration as part of the acquisition process. process (Tempest et al., 2000)[1]

"The due diligence process was also carried out with integration in mind. It served the company in assessing the different aspects of the target such as talent, technology, management and financing, all of which were aimed at validating the selection decision and facilitating later integration. Indeed, the two keys for successful acquisition, namely selection and integration, were strongly tied to a thorough due diligence process. To ensure the success of its acquisitions, Cisco's integration process was focused on three goals – in descending order of importance: (1) employee retention; (2) follow-up on new product development; and (3) return on investment." (Brueller & Capron, 2010)[2]

Cisco has since changed this strategy and has led to speculation about its sometimes unsuccessful integrations of companies like IronPort, that was very focused on its top talent. The IronPort CEO admittedly struggled to integrate Cisco people with his staff due to culture clashes and a lack of preparation and consideration of these issues before the deal was done. (Weiss, 2013)[3]

1: Tempest N, Kasper C, Wheelwright S, Holloway C. 2000. Cisco Systems, Inc.: Acquisition integration for manufacturing. Harvard Business School, Case No. 9-600-015, February 15.

2: (INSEAD Business Case: Cisco Systems: New Millennium – New Acquisition Strategy?)

3: (https://scott.a16z.com/2013/02/06/the-i-just-got-bought-by-a-big-company-survival-guide/, INSEAD Case)

Preparation in this sense is about more than just integration design. Thorough preparation is aimed not only at pushing the integration agenda forwards, but also at creating a fertile environment and giving people the psychological edge needed see the integration through. This is done in three important ways. First, recognising the importance of culture in any M&A deal, essentially by understanding the behaviours that drive your company's and the target's performance. Second, embedding accountability at the onset, ensuring those driving the deal will be held accountable for delivering the benefits. Finally, by generating a sense of momentum and support by engaging all stakeholders throughout the process.

To integrate or not to integrate

Approaches to integration should be tailored to the benefits you are trying to achieve and the operating model changes you need to make. Although we've focused on full integration, this is not always the right or best answer. Sometimes only particular elements of a company need to be integrated, and, on rare occasions, they should be left alone completely.

When a business is purchased because of a core capability – such as a sophisticated technology or R&D department – it is sometimes the case that the acquiring culture differs significantly with the group that delivers this capability. In this scenario, fully integrating such a capability would limit or destroy its utility. The classic archetype of this is when (creative, cool, agile and fun) content companies meet (efficient, solid, boring but reliable) platform companies – anyone mention Time Warner/AOL? Industries in which products or services are still rapidly evolving tend to be fully integrated so as to control the innovation process. However, when the products or services are more standardised, companies seek increased efficiency by outsourcing these functions.

When full integration goes wrong

As part of a manufacturing business integration, it was decided to roll out the acquiring firm's mature ERP system to the acquired site, imposing a fundamentally different system and way of working onto a finance team comprising three individuals used to working with spreadsheets. While well-intended, the result was a seven-month implementation project costing over half a million dollars delivering an unnecessarily-complex solution with little material benefit in evidence.

On other occasions, a more nuanced approach may be more appropriate. Selected processes could be 'imposed' upon the acquired company, while retaining the independence of the front office functions if the markets they serve are distinct. In one example, a facilities management business using an outdated bespoke software package to manage their customer interactions acquired a software firm in the sector to transform its service to customers and reduce cost. Unsurprisingly, the culture of the acquired software team was radically different to that of the buyer, so a full integration that still retained critical staff on both sides would have been complex if not outright impossible. Instead, integration focused on the replacement of the old software with the new across the combined customer base, while leaving much of both legacy organisations untouched.

Knowing thyself is the beginning of all wisdom (Aristotle)

You are buying a company or set of assets for what they can add to your business and the combined entity. You're looking for scale or new products, access to new customers or markets, a new set of skills. This implies being open to what the new company can bring and perhaps even flexible in how you incorporate aspects of the target business into yours. You can't be dogmatic about how things will be done, lest you lose the very advantage you are paying for – sound familiar?

Well, yes and no. Before you can open your mind – and your organisation – to new ways of approaching things, you need to understand what you're not willing to compromise on, otherwise you inadvertently give up what has made your company successful in the first place. What do *you* bring to the table in this deal? What will make *you* the best owner of this asset/business in the market?

Hence, a necessary condition for successful integrations is knowing what makes your own organisation successful – now and into the future. What are the elements of your own strategy, operating model, skill base, human asset profile and strategy, culture and other key building blocks which you are not willing to compromise on? What are the enduring values, principles and behaviours that define your business and that you are determined will need to find their way into the combined organisation?

In sum, are there any non-negotiables in the way that you will operate your business in the future that must be commuted to the new organisation – reporting standards, levels of accountability and transparency, the way customers are treated or communities are managed?

Only once you have established these immutable elements can you confidently move forward and incorporate new approaches. Identifying and articulating these immutable elements is an important task in the early integration design, allowing you to move into the integration execution – and even the pre-close negotiations – with confidence. We will see later how this preparatory work will also stand you in good stead to set out your stall clearly and confidently early in the post-close environment.

Equally important is the need to objectively assess your own organisation's ability to 'digest' the new acquisition. Immature or sub-scale internal processes and systems may mean that as a business you're not yet truly 'growth ready': Are your finance systems able to accommodate a wider range of products, customers and – for international acquisitions – accounting? Is your culture well-suited to running a larger business? Are your key people ready to take on more responsibility? It's true that in some cases the acquisition itself may bring in the very capabilities you need to address these issues, provided you're ready and willing for the significant changes that might be required in your own business to make this work.

Know the target company, understand the transaction

"If you know the enemy and know yourself, you need not fear the result of a hundred battles." Sun Tsu

Pursuing a transaction is exciting, sometimes becoming a distraction from the drudgery or difficulty of managing the current business. While an enticing opportunity, transactions put organisations at enhanced risk, destabilise the core business and place a strain on its employees and relationships with all stakeholders. The answer to the question "considering all the potential benefits and risks, is my shareholders' money well spent on this transaction?" must be unequivocally positive before one embarks on such a risky endeavour. This is equally true when considering what is best for the company as a whole and other key groups who are also impacted by the risk and reward of the deal (e.g. employees, the local community, customers).

The answer of course emerges largely from the analytical work that is being performed in preparation for a transaction and, of course, in due diligence. However, traditional due diligence falls way short of answering the question comprehensively and honestly. A thorough understanding of the target company in the context of the practical execution of the combination, the ongoing operations, mitigation of risks and capturing of opportunities is invaluable in providing the confidence that the upheaval is indeed warranted.

So, starting early *is* the foundation for a successful integration, helping to foster the right kind of mentality and psychology. If people do not feel sufficiently prepared, motivated or ready for an integration process, minor challenges can become insurmountable.

Take culture seriously

Executives rarely abort a transaction due to concerns about the challenges of post-deal integration, or the potential incompatibility of company cultures. More often, the desire to complete transactions, encouraged by advisors and others incentivised to close a deal, leads to underplaying the risks of combining two entities with inevitably unique characteristics and idiosyncrasies. After all, there is value in the differences, right?

Not when it comes to culture. After all, your organisation's culture is the set of heuristics and behaviours that define *how* you go about your business.

Time and again, culture, in one form or another, is cited as the biggest contributor to acquisition failure. Heralded at the time as a 'merger between equals', the Daimler-Benz/Chrysler combination now serves as one of the most prominent examples of the failure to recognise the perils of cultural dissonance (BBC, 1998)[4]. From brand philosophy to the people and processes themselves, numerous reports have surfaced of both overt and underlying tension. Tuck School of Business described how Chrysler's brand value lay in its 'assertiveness and risk-taking cowboy aura, all produced within a cost-controlled atmosphere. Mercedes-Benz, in contrast, exuded disciplined German engineering coupled with uncompromising quality' (Finkelstein, 2002)[5].

Fundamental differences were said to have led to underlying tensions between the companies. Solomon & Schell describe Ray Wilhelm, a manager at Chrysler, and his experience at a brainstorming meeting with colleagues from Daimler-Benz. Stark differences quickly became apparent when the Germans drafted a 40-slide presentation with detailed proposals, while

---

4: News.bbc.co.uk. (1998). BBC News | Business | Daimler, Chrysler confirm merger. [online] Available at: http://news.bbc.co.uk/1/hi/business/88912.stm [Accessed 25 Jan. 2019].

5: Finkelstein S. (2002). The DaimlerChrysler Merger. Tuck School of Business at Dartmouth.

the Americans expected to start from scratch. "The Germans seemed to disapprove of the Americans' lack of preparation. This reduced collaboration and led to a rift." (Solomon & Schell, 2009)[6].

Michael Watkins concluded that "efforts to integrate the operations of Daimler and Chrysler foundered on lack of trust clashes", due to "unbridgeable differences in the cultures of the two organizations" (Watkins, 2007)[7]. A year after the merger, one third of Chrysler's senior managers had quit. By 2007, Daimler-Benz sold Chrysler for $6bn, a $44bn loss (Solomon & Schell, 2009).

Could this have been avoided? We can never be sure, but reports imply that more could have been done to check the viability of cultural integration. In particular, one of the Daimler managers involved in the pre-merger discussions, told the Economist that 'questions raised by the deal's cross-border nature were not specifically asked until after its broad terms had been agreed' (The Economist, 2000)[8].

And this challenge isn't getting any easier: Kraft's acquisition

---

6: Solomon, C. and Schell, M. (2009). Managing across cultures. New York: McGraw-Hill

7: Watkins, M. (2007). Why DaimlerChrysler Never Got into Gear. [online] Harvard Business Review. Available at: https://hbr.org/2007/05/why-the-daimlerchrysler-merger [Accessed 25 Jan. 2019].

8: The Economist. (2000). The DaimlerChrysler emulsion. [online] Available at: https://www.economist.com/briefing/2000/07/27/the-daimlerchrysler-emulsion [Accessed 25 Jan. 2019].

of Cadbury[9] in 2010 is a more recent example of culture 'eating M&A for breakfast', but conversely Microsoft has been recently cited for a significant positive cultural change, driven at least in part through its acquisition of businesses such as Skype and LinkedIn.

Kraft's hostile takeover of Cadbury

In 2010, US food company Kraft successfully completed its hostile takeover of UK's Cadbury after two years of contentious negotiation, protests and battles. The deal demonstrates an inherent culture clash between a corporate giant and a family business with a distinct brand heritage committed to social good. Kraft was accused of going back on promises made to retain factories and commit to maintaining Cadbury's practice of using Fairtrade cocoa beans. Could these issues have been better considered pre-close and better managed in the first months after the deal? We believe so.

So, here's the takeaway: don't let cultural challenges go by unaddressed. Understand your own and the target company's cultures (and there may be more than two!), and be honest

---

9: Morris, S. (2010). Cadbury workers protest against takeover. [online] the Guardian. Available at: https://www.theguardian.com/business/2010/jan/27/cadburyworkers-takeover-protest [Accessed 25 Jan. 2019].

Fearn, H. (2016). In a final betrayal of the Cadbury brand, Kraft has quietly abandoned its promise to stick with Fairtrade. [online] The Independent. Available at: https://www.independent.co.uk/voices/cadburys-chocolate-fairtrade-fair-trade-mark-farmers-kraftamerican-brand-abandoned-promise-a7445826.html [Accessed 25 Jan. 2019].

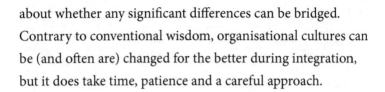

about whether any significant differences can be bridged. Contrary to conventional wisdom, organisational cultures can be (and often are) changed for the better during integration, but it does take time, patience and a careful approach.

Pick your A-Team

Choosing the right people for the due diligence and integration team is key to ensuring the right questions are asked and the right experienced-based insights will be generated. As discussed in more detail later it is also critical to ensuring that the right level of accountability is built into everything that follows, from benefits targets to valuation to integration planning and execution.

In the first instance, the selection of the integration director is a pivotal decision. Too often the person responsible for integration is a young staffer with time on their hands. While there are many useful roles such individuals can play, taking overall responsibility for the entire process and its deliverables is rarely one of them. Integration is one of the most complex, pressured, entrepreneurial activities an organisation can undertake. It is risky and unpredictable. The role requires rapid decision-making, an ability to deal with uncertainty and risk and the skill to drive a predefined plan; while being able to change course if circumstance requires. Moreover, the role cuts across functions and operations, head office and operating boundaries and extends to external stakeholders. The leader must be comfortable working across and within boundaries, maintaining momentum and gaining commitment *without* the formal authority afforded by a normal organisation structure. This is the reason an integration director should – for the duration of the integration – be visibly granted the same level of authority as the senior-most operating executive that will be affected. To quote a major pharmaceutical company integration leader a few years ago, "Despite what seems to be the case around here, availability should *not* be considered a core skill when choosing an integration manager!" An excellent guide to the role and characteristics of M&A and integration leadership can be found in *Harvard Business Review's* Integration Managers: Special Leaders for Special Times (HBR, November 2000), and in The Leaders Who Make M&A Work (HBR, September 2014).

You will have guessed that the integration director is someone who can least afford to take time out from a pressurised role. They also need some specific skills beyond operating experience. They should be a good programme (not just project) manager and have a thorough understanding of your company, the processes and values, what's important and how you go about your business. They need to be decisive and to be able to drive – no, accelerate – the process of integration.

They should be able to hold their own in the executive board and amongst executives who, until now, may have been more senior.

If you don't find a person that fits this, your integration will be off to a poor start, significantly increasing the chances of failure.

Where do we find such rare animals? Scrutinise your high-flyer list – this is an ideal learning opportunity for a next-generation operating executive. Look amongst your Second in Commands and next level of operating managers. Here you will find your gem.

A final word of caution on the integration director: ambitious high-flyers are clearly valuable members of the organisation and the integration experience will make them even more so. Their career path post-integration should be clear and discussed with them prior to commencing their role as integration director. Too often one sees an integration manager leave the organisation because they cannot find a role back in the main structure, occasionally exacerbated by changes in their own expectations. Good integration managers typically make excellent general managers, and often use the experience as a springboard to a senior leadership role within your business…or someone else's.

Who else is in the team?

This depends on the structure of your integration process which, in turn, is driven by the physical functions and assets that require integration. Typically, there are two types of integration teams – functional and operating. The operating teams are responsible for integrating specific assets, business units, product groups or the like. Functional teams have two roles – to integrate their own functions (finance, IT, legal, marketing, etc.) and to provide the operating teams with specific functional support. Additionally, the integration exercise requires an integration steering committee, populated by at least the CEO, CFO and integration director, plus the relevant operating executives. The steering committee's role is to monitor the integration, to set the key principles, to make the key decisions and, where required, to remove obstacles to success. Additionally, the integration director may have their own project management team which could include one or more integration project managers, depending on the size of the integration challenge. Finally the importance of building and sustaining internal and external engagement and support throughout the integration is reflected in the positioning of an 'engagement and communications team' alongside the steering committee. The diagram below is a generic illustration of how an integration activity can be structured:

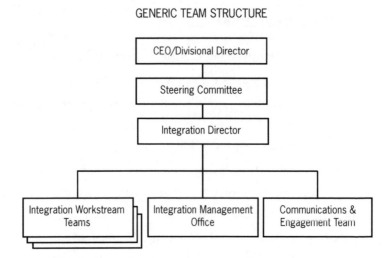

GENERIC TEAM STRUCTURE

While this integration structure – tailored to the idiosyncrasies and scale of the integration effort in question – comes into its own around the time the transaction closes, it is important to set it up early in the due diligence process and populate it with those who are essential to integration due diligence, design and planning.

For example, someone from HR will help to define the target's organisation structure, identify the target's employees who must be retained (the 'keepers'), map out the remuneration and other HR policies, evaluate the pension arrangements, gain a sense of the vital cultural components, and so on. Similarly, someone from treasury, IT, legal or finance will need to perform a similar evaluation of the target and begin to generate hypotheses about how the combination may work. These individuals should also help define their relevant integration targets, feeding them into the entire due diligence process by sharing information from their function that may affect others. Numerous options exist for teams to share this information – from ensuring the different functions come together regularly, to simply passing relevant information to a centralised team. However this is achieved, it is vital to recognise that the different functions are likely to uncover complex information that may affect other functions in ways that might not be immediately visible. Therefore, the team structure and processes should be designed and populated in advance to encourage this behaviour, and the methods and lines of communication clearly identified.

Cross-functional sharing

During a 'simple' due diligence exercise for a $200m acquisition, several post-close problems related to HR policies and practices were identified...by the legal DD team. Rather than leaving their findings to be buried in their final report, they were immediately shared with the HR team, who were then able to assess and plan their integration activities appropriately.

Sizing your integration team to match the scale and complexity of the target is another important decision. If the financial controller in the target company also takes care of treasury, tax, board reporting and investor relations, then populating your team with one person for each of these individual functions will sound alarm bells about your culture and your intentions for the target company. Are you bureaucratic? Are you heavy handed? Are you overly centralised? In such a case, amalgamate numerous functions under a single individual responsible for their integration.

You are now at a juncture at which executive judgement is required. Designing and populating an integration team structure so long before the deal is consummated has its challenges, not least of which is securing sufficient time from the individuals in question – and their bosses – and maintaining their interest through what can often be a protracted pre-deal period.

At the same time, it is important not to over-involve the proposed team leaders and others prior to the close as transactions can break down at any time. The key is striking the balance between being prepared *vs*. disrupting the core business. Reviewing and adjusting the level of commitment of the integration team at each milestone of the transaction can help guard against under- or over-commitment. Integration teams must also be incentivised to focus on specifically assigned integration objectives to maintain this balance.

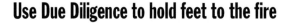

Use Due Diligence to hold feet to the fire

Due Diligence rarely plays a big enough role in integration planning, even when correctly seen as the primary connection between M&A and the integration itself. Without the right people involved, or the right objectives and mentality permeating the process, the true value of due diligence for integration purposes is rarely extracted.

Typically, due diligence includes various types of analysis directed at determining whether the target business is the right opportunity, identifying potential reasons for not doing the transaction ('deal killers'), or obstacles to closing a transaction, opportunities for synergies or extracting value once the business is acquired and, of course, valuing the business. While synergy analysis is performed – and in the best cases, it is based on a strategic and commercial analysis of the combination – this synergy analysis can suffer from two significant shortcomings.

First, those performing the analysis – advisors or internal corporate finance teams – often have no responsibility for (or experience in) delivering the result. Worse, their incentive can be perverse – to inflate the synergy number to substantiate a transaction from which they may stand to benefit, even if only indirectly. Second, the process of determining a 'synergy number' seldom includes a fundamental analysis of the integration steps required to deliver the synergies, or of the risks associated with each activity; and, hence, the probability of achieving the component numbers. As much as you can, determine the value of synergies bottom-up based on facts; not top-down, based on assumptions or prior precedent.

Traditional due diligence can also be plagued by a lack of objectivity, which typically presents itself in one of two forms. The first is 'deal fever', the process whereby all work is geared towards validating a decision already made by the leadership to buy a company. If this unspoken message becomes known, all processes established to test the hypothesis will find themselves compelled to support the leadership. The second is 'deal momentum', where the board, management, employees and advisors invest so much time and political capital in the deal that they are equally motivated to ensure it goes through. Warning signs are rationalised away or purposely overlooked ("If everyone else is convinced, sticking my neck out will only harm me."), and consequently the deal will be pursued even when common sense would suggest a different path should be taken.

Promoting accountability helps to fix these defects. Best practice demands that the transaction due diligence process is enhanced through the incorporation of a substantial integration due diligence component from the outset (for an excellent example of this see the CISCO acquisition strategy evolution and IronPort deal of 2007. It provides a valuable lesson in adequate pre-deal preparation and cultural evaluation[10]). This is really no more complex than asking 'drill-down' questions. If a synergy has been identified around a projected increase in sales, ask yourself, "What products? Where, and with which customer groups? What would it take to achieve this; more volume, a higher price, or both? How would any volume increase be achieved? What changes to sales team structure, incentives, training or support would this require?" Get to the heart of the assumption, and don't let go until you are satisfied the goal is realistic and achievable, because you are confident in the 'how' behind the 'what'. This necessarily implies the involvement of those in the organisation who have the best knowledge of functions or operations from which the synergies will stem and, *importantly*, who are likely to be responsible for delivering them. Consequently, far more attention will be directed to post-acquisition integration challenges, risks and opportunities.

Without the early involvement of those responsible for the execution of the integration, accountability is diluted or, worse, non-existent from the start. Managers who miss targets or fail to achieve their integration goals will quickly complain that they were not involved in setting them and that they were unachievable in the first place. "I could have told you, but you

---

10: Regan, K. (2007). Cisco Buys IronPort for $830 Million. [online] E-commerce Times. Available at: https://www.ecommercetimes.com/story/54992.html [Accessed 25 Jan. 2019].

never asked!" is all too common post-close…and completely avoidable.

Naturally, this process can lead to the opposite bias – the desire to be conservative, to under-promise and over-deliver. The consequent under-estimation of the potential synergies can impact the ability to compete for a target and is a bias that needs to be counterbalanced by senior executives involved in the final bid evaluation. The CEO and CFO should counterbalance the risk of being overly conservative by critically scrutinising the estimates for padding and conservatism. Accountability extends beyond the internal functional and operating teams to all stakeholders – the executive team, the board, key shareholders, anyone who you need to keep with you throughout the complex and fraught process of pursuing and integrating a transaction.

Starting the integration planning process early – and including the key stakeholders in the relevant discussions of how the companies will come together – will help engender support, but also allows the CEO and integration leaders to create accountability early on. No excuses, no volte faces, no back-tracking.

Manage the role of consultants

Consultants, in one form or another, will usually play a role. Integration is not an everyday activity and additional capacity and specific skills will be required which most organisations typically cannot afford to keep on the permanent payroll. However, returning to the key success factor of accountability, consultants cannot be expected to be accountable for the business – now or in the future. Inserting consultants into roles which should be performed by line management not only confuses and jeopardises decision making but runs the risk of emasculating the line managers themselves; it can make them under-responsible and disengaged; it can be obstructive and counter-productive. The role of the consultant can be to manage or facilitate the process, support project and line managers, provide a constant drumbeat to ensure the right things are happening at pace, and challenge conventional thinking so that the right questions are being asked. They can provide frameworks, templates and tools to ease the mechanics of the process. They can nudge, remind, analyse and synthesise. They can also bring specialist expertise – for example, in IT, where the internal team may lack the knowledge of the target company's IT infrastructure or, indeed, of how to integrate them. What they cannot do is run the business or ensure the deal succeeds. Even in the most technically taxing situations, overall and ultimate accountability must remain with the internal executives. Above all, if the situation warrants a consultant it is vital they are truly committed to the relationship, not just the transaction.

Carry all your stakeholders…right from the start

As conventional best practice for integration will tell you, communicate, communicate, communicate and communicate again. This mantra will permeate every aspect of your post-deal activities. One cannot overestimate the amount of communication that is required to reduce uncertainty, distraction and build support – it is the bedrock of any successful integration. What the books don't tell you is that it begins pre-deal, typically with due diligence.

M&A can be a very effective path towards growth but is also an unpredictable endeavour with an unenviable track record of failure. It is unsettling to even the most confident. Scepticism is the knee-jerk response and detractors have their ways of distancing themselves and perhaps even resisting a transaction. The path will inevitably be rocky – integration is equal parts opportunity and risk, and the right balance needs to be struck. It is therefore important to generate and maintain support of key stakeholders. A failure to constantly communicate will leave the executive suite and key employees disenchanted and lacking in motivation, board members dubious, and shareholders considering a quick exit. Meanwhile, the uncertainty that can ensue will be exploited by competitors looking for weaknesses and distraction, and convincing your customers, suppliers and employees that their best option will be to switch allegiances.

Stakeholder involvement

Relevant stakeholders are different in every deal, but they inevitably go beyond your own company. Here are two prominent examples:

- *Customers:* For B2B companies, it can be important (once the deal is announced) to talk to customers as they can become anxious that prices will go up, service will go down, or even that the increased supplier concentration (you!) will pose too great a risk to their business. Only through effective communications will you prevent customers from leaving as a direct result of the deal.

- *Potential employees:* Left to their own devices, the media can drive a negative perception of the acquiring or combined business, highlighting problems over successes. Employee-driven company rating sites can also reinforce any negative perception of the company if internal stress and uncertainty exists. Proactive measures can help you retain your ability to recruit top talent post-close, at just the time when you may need it most. Communication to your employment market plays a large part in this.

Communication requires planning, proactivity and responsiveness. Identify all the relevant stakeholders – internal and external – and map their potential communication needs at each step of the transaction process, from due diligence through completion…and beyond. Try to anticipate their anxieties and questions and prepare focused communication plans for each stakeholder at each phase of the process.

But even early pre-close, it is especially important to manage your board and your internal executives carefully. Prepare for a potential leak of the transaction and have holding statements, key messaging and Q&As in place. Anticipate the needs and interests of regulators and your shareholders – irrespective of whether you're a public or private company. The CEO's role is to keep the constituencies aligned as the transaction meanders towards its conclusion. It is a very common mistake to assume that everyone will share your enthusiasm for the transaction. The most pertinent question is 'What does it mean for me?' and everyone is asking this from the moment the acquisition is mooted, pre-close or post. If the there is no common, formal narrative that addresses this question, it will be answered through conjecture, rumour and water-cooler gossip. Productivity will fall, anxiety will escalate and you will lose support for your transaction – visibly or more insidiously.

Go further. Once you are certain that the transaction is the correct course of action for the organisation and for shareholders, create a coalition of support. The trick here is to identify the key individuals who can help disseminate their enthusiasm and support for the deal throughout the company (as and when considerations around confidentiality allow).

The primary focus here will inevitably be on the C-Suite, but there are also three individuals of note who will need particular attention. The CFO will be relied upon to ensure the deal makes financial sense for the company and can be financed. The Head of M&A or Head of Strategy is again essential as they will run the deal process. Finally, the chosen business unit leaders, who will run the combined business units, will need to support the deal whole-heartedly, and be willing to advocate its benefits throughout the organisation.

And don't forget the most important group of all – your board. We've seen multiple cases over the years where board support is lazily assumed to be in place, or arrogantly assumed to be easily managed. This can result in deals being rejected at the last minute, leading to wasted time, effort and money, damaged careers, and acrimony within the business. Make absolutely certain that the strategy is clear, and that this acquisition 'makes sense' to each and every board member. Set and closely monitor expectations upfront. Tell your board how they should assess the success of the transaction and then report against those metrics. You are in a unique position to determine the criteria and expectations which will determine the real – and perceived – success or failure of a transaction. Define these carefully and then provide these key stakeholders with a scorecard against which to measure you and the transaction's success. This, of course, harbours the risk of being hoisted by one's own petard, but it is preferable to being measured against some spurious, unpredictable and often irrelevant and uninfluenceable metrics.

KEY CONCEPTS:

1. Start early but manage the pace and expectations.

2. Take culture seriously – don't paper over the differences.

3. Know your company, what makes you successful and what is immutable.

4. Know the target; become intimate with your target and how it operates.

5. Pick the A-team:

   a. Focus on selecting the right Integration Director;

   b. Structure the team to match the scale and complexity of the target.

6. Never dilute accountability:

   a. Manage executive biases to facilitate the making of rational decisions;

   b. Combine transaction and integration due diligence into a seamless process that enhances accountability;

   c. Manage the role of consultants as facilitators and advisers, not owners of ultimate benefits delivery.

7. Don't leave any stakeholders behind pre-close, especially the board – communicate relentlessly.

Chapter 2:
BUSINESS IS WAR... BUT WHAT ABOUT THE PEACE?

"Rather than comparing war to art we could more accurately compare it to commerce, which is also a conflict of human interests and activities."

CARL VON CLAUSEWITZ – ON WAR, BOOK I, CH. 3

"Deal negotiations had been hard. Both sides walked away from the table at least once, sometimes as a calculated bluff, sometimes for real. The lawyers had certainly earned their money, striking an aggressive tone with Lidare's management team and pushing for the best deal they could for Quintado. They got it too, despite a bruising three weeks of negotiations. Given the problems and additional cost he was now facing, Paul was glad to have some additional wiggle room in his Business Case; a higher deal price would have made his targets even harder to reach.

They also managed to lock down Jason, Lidare's VP of R&D, the mastermind of their core software product, and the real diamond that made Lidare such an important acquisition. OK, so he and Jason had never really seen eye to eye, and this was a real obstacle pre-deal, but the right mix of hard truths around exactly what would be done with his team post-close, an obscene retention package, and the occasional reminder that Quintado now owned his brainchild, left Jason no choice but to cave. Good thing too: several months in, it was even clearer to Paul that Jason's team were the drones serving the one queen bee: everything rested on Jason's ability to design and deliver the next release on schedule."

Business can be a brutal enterprise, conventionally perceived as a zero-sum game. This mindset is no more evident than in M&A, in which the objective is often simply to 'get the best deal possible for the company'. During the negotiation phase, securing the best terms remains the focus: us against you; our shareholders' interests against yours. During integration, we will seek every opportunity to cut costs, increase efficiency and deliver the identified synergies. Sound logical?

The notion of a 'winner' and a 'loser' in a transaction is further reinforced by the public discourse, particularly in a merger. Speculation begins on which company's CEO and CFO will survive, what the board composition is likely to be, the name of the new company, and so on.

Herein lies the rub. The conduct of the deal team and the principals aggressively negotiating the transaction often sets the tone for the post-deal relationships. Not only can it govern the way the integration is perceived, or indeed, its very success, but, in the extreme, can colour the long-term relationship between the acquiring team and target company's employees and stakeholders as a whole. First impressions count, and these form well before Day One.

While the desire to maximise the spoils seems intuitive and even essential, treating M&A purely as combat ignores the potential psychological impacts on post-deal dynamics. Time and time again negotiations deteriorate into aggressive, bad-natured power struggles. Look at any textbook on deal negotiations and you'll find many standard tactics that may be helpful for winning the best deal, but destroy relationships along the way. Unlike many other negotiations, M&A represents the start of a relationship, not the end. The tactics utilised to get what seems to be the best deal at the time can ultimately create an image of a company that is domineering and nasty.[1] The contentious public battle between Vodafone and Mannesmann in the late 1990s serves as a cautionary tale of how detrimental it can be to carry that emotional baggage into a post-deal integration process. Such a reputation can seriously hinder integration, or even consign it to failure before it starts.

1: Saigol, L. (2013). Vodafone aims to banish ghosts of acquisitions past I Financial Times. [online] Ft.com. Available at: https://www.ft.com/content/7ead3928-d342-11e2-b3ff-00144feab7de [Accessed 25 Jan. 2019].

Vodafone's public acquisition battle with Mannesmann

In what was widely regarded as a war of words, the CEOs of UK's Vodafone and Germany's Mannessmann used the press to make jabs at one another, taking their acquisition battle to the streets. While Mannessmann was convincing its stakeholders that they would be better off on their own, Vodafone was doing its own backchanneling to secure stakeholder support. When Mannessman realised resistance was futile and reluctantly agreed to the deal, the remnants of the public battle remained while the companies attempted to integrate. Five years later, Vodafone made one of its biggest post-acquisition writedowns to date to compensate for deal losses.

Skilled acquirers strike the balance between achieving the optimal deal, while keeping an eye on the future as it relates to current or inherited stakeholders. The target company should emerge from negotiations with its reputation intact, the combination viewed as an attractive place to work, and with both sides contemplating a positive future together.

The imperative for serial acquirers to pay attention to their image is even higher. The best of them are cognisant of their overall image as a buyer well beyond the current transaction. For them, one integration is simply part of a longer journey. Their reputation is constructed deal by deal, making it more difficult – and more important – to sustain a positive image.

How exactly is this Gordian Knot cut?

Test your mental models

In October 1962, a period of thirteen days came close to altering the course of human history. The Cuban Missile Crisis – as it became known in the Western world – put the world on the brink of nuclear war, one which the Pentagon estimated would directly kill over 150 million people (even before taking into account the after-effects of radiation). This state of tension came about because of – and was later avoided due to a change in – the mental models each party had of their adversaries. Bruce Allyn's book, 'The Edge of Armageddon: Lessons from the Brink', details the influence of the perception Americans, Cubans and Russians had of each other and of their motives and modi operandi, and how these varying perspectives led to such an escalation. Reportedly, the crisis was diffused and nuclear disaster averted as a result of President John F. Kennedy's insightful unwillingness to interpret certain critical events through the lens of the US hawks' simplistic mental model of a centrally-controlled Soviet Union.

This historic event holds direct lessons for M&A and its potential post-deal impacts. How many times have you heard someone on the deal team say, "Those guys are playing games", "they can't be trusted", or similar? It is common, and particularly damaging, for parties negotiating a transaction –

especially public transactions or those where there has been limited contact between the firms – to develop strong mental models of each player, together with all the inherent biases that go with such generalisations. "These guys always renege on the commitments they make" or "they will fight for the last cent" or, worse still for post-merger integration, "they always fire the top executives and shut down the corporate offices of companies they acquire". Every subsequent action and behaviour is interpreted through the lens of the mental model held at the time, often leading to inappropriate and unintended conclusions that manifest themselves in resistance, mistrust and fear.

Instead, put yourself in the other party's shoes; understand their concerns. The target's owners and business leaders will rightly be concerned about their jobs, their legacy, their teams, and their personal reputations: Will my people like working for this group once I'm gone? What will my peers think of me if I concede this point? Do I like and respect these people enough to want to work with them in the future? What will this deal mean for my career opportunities? Very standard 'what about me' questions that need to be applied to those on the other side of the negotiating table just as much to your employees post-announcement. Understanding their personal motivations beyond the deal itself will not only improve chances of long-term success, it will also give you an edge during the negotiations themselves.

The view from their side: first impressions count

'Us against them' is an axiom that tends to run through most negotiations and public conversations before and sometimes even during an integration. Naturally it is believed that the best way to deliver the most value from a deal is to start with securing the lowest price. Acquirers often forget, however, that every move they make helps others to gradually construct an image of their organisation and what it will be like to work with them – or more accurately, for them.

While your company is going to great lengths to build a mental model of the target organisation, the target organisation (consciously or subconsciously) is doing the same with you. The difference is that they will create this depiction of you based on any accessible information – including how you're interacting with them, what you're saying to the press, any reports you've released, and what the media said about your last deal – but may not go to the same lengths as you to investigate and validate their assumptions. Consequently, it is critically important to create an impression in line with your desired post-acquisition story. Getting the very best deal can mean little if you generate such a poor perception of your company and intentions that target executives and staff become antipathetic to the incoming change; or even openly hostile, as was the case with Vodafone and Mannesmann.

Send the right smoke signals

In the bravado of a transaction, every action, word, legal exchange or public statement carries the potential for misinterpretation and manipulation by those keen to create their own picture of the deal.

So, while the deal team is negotiating the best outcome for its shareholders, other mechanisms must be utilised to deliver a new, engaging and exciting vision of the post-deal future. Over the cacophony of lawyers, investment bankers and business development counterparts, the execution of a premeditated communications plan is essential to delivering a vision for the combined entity; a clear set of messages on how the target fits into the overall strategy of a stronger, more competitive combined entity – all without compromising the ongoing negotiations.

The recipients for these messages and vision are multifarious – extending well beyond the target company's management, board and shareholders to, among others: national regulators approving the transaction; local authorities who influence future investment plans; industry groups who control licenses to operate; community interest groups wishing to protect local areas or practices; trade unions who can see transactions as an opportunity to regain lost ground or reset relationships.

Every meeting, press statement, regulatory filing or

stakeholder interaction – no matter how informal – serves as an opportunity to build this new, positive picture; or alternatively, to entrench an already unfavourable one.

At the same time, and with a view to preserving the acquirer's integrity amongst key stakeholders, false or uncertain promises must be avoided. They *will* come back to haunt you.

Building a successful business is a long game and the internet never forgets!

Even though it took place in the late 1990s, the troubles between Vodafone and Mannesmann during their acquisition and integration live on through the magic of the internet. To work around this problem, bear these two important points in mind as negotiations unfold: first, that every conversation is an integration discussion; and, second, your reputation can precede you if left unmanaged. Transaction negotiations double up as opportunities to manage the post-deal discourse and to shape the mental picture the target is developing of your company, and of the combined future together.

Every conversation is an integration discussion

Too often, conversations – or, more precisely, negotiations – with counterparts from a target company (or merger partner) are conducted in a completely different manner from those you intend to have once the transaction is closed. This is not only true of your own executives and staff, your press and corporate affairs team, but also of your advisors. While they may be focused on the negotiation, the counterparties are thinking about the implications for them as a company and, more often, as individuals working for or with you. Heavy-handed and uncompromising discussions pre-close will colour impressions, making the integration itself an uphill battle from the start.

The negotiation discourse – both content and style – will impact plans for post-close and, in turn, could impact the negotiations themselves: "If this is going to be a nasty place to work after the deal, we better secure an even better deal for our shareholders, and ourselves, while we still can".

How do you want them to feel about you?

First, there needs to be a compelling narrative about the logic of the transaction and the strategy and prospects of the combined entity. Then, key messages and Q&As must be developed addressing hypothetical queries by the counterparty's representatives. These messages form the basis of all the transaction-related communications – whether they are by the advisors to their counterparts, or executive to executive, through the media or even to external stakeholders like local and national governments, trade unions and local communities. Without damaging the prospects of achieving an optimal transaction, you must communicate your 'deal narrative' in a consistent and clear manner to all stakeholders via all the potential channels, including third-party advisors interacting on your behalf. For example, significant attention should be paid to deal announcements sharing your key messages with the public. In announcing the $19bn acquisition of WhatsApp in February 2014, Facebook's Mark Zuckerberg said "WhatsApp is on a path to connect one billion people. The services that reach that milestone are all incredibly valuable. I've known Jan (Koum, founder and CEO) for a long time and I'm excited to partner with him and his team to make the world more open and connected." Positive, but lacking in any detail regarding the 'why' or the 'how' of the deal. The result? On releasing this announcement, Facebook's share price immediately dropped 3.4%, instantly wiping close to $6 billion off their value.

Here's where a simple mistake is often made – in an attempt to keep costs down, legal and other teams are rarely brought in early, or briefed on the broader deal rationale and interpersonal aspects that have preceded their involvement. "Just go in and drive a hard bargain" is often where it all begins. Instead, make sure your legal, PR and banking teams are aware and sensitive to your culture, longer-term objectives, what you've learned about the individuals on the other side of the table and your plans for these people *before* they get involved and unintentionally undo months of relationship building. That doesn't prevent them from playing hard cop on your behalf, but it does allow them to do so more carefully and effectively.

Beyond the narrative, the style of interaction must also be co-ordinated. Decide what aspects of your culture you wish to emphasise and weave these into your interactions with the other side. Are you collaborative, decisive or results-oriented? Are you ambitious about the company's role in the industry, or govern your business by a set of hard values? Are you focused on cost, revenue, profit or share price? Mirror these attributes in your interactions and communicate them through the key messages you share with your team. There's no point turning up in a fleet of limousines before sharing your strategic vision to be the low-cost producer in the industry. If you wish to promote a decisive, action-oriented culture, don't prevaricate.

Many organisations go further, intentionally 'dialling up' their own presentation of their values and culture in their interactions with the target, working hard to make sure they understand the kind of organisation they would be joining. Speak openly about the things that your leaders see as important, 'red lines', typical behaviours, and the history that led to them. Your observation of their reaction to this conversation will also help you decide if this deal is actually going to work, over and above what your spreadsheets may tell you.

At the same time, creating false expectations about job

security, or the maintenance of the investment budget, or of offices or facilities, is equally dangerous. It is especially tricky when it comes to commitments being made to regulators, which are often documents of public record – especially in cross-border transactions. Reassuring regulators that you will not adopt a scorched-earth policy post-close has to be counterbalanced with the risk of creating a false sense of security amongst the staff or other stakeholders (e.g. local communities) about employment, investments or facilities. Undoing these false impressions once the transaction has closed will destroy your credibility, prove traumatic for all parties and guarantee a poor start for the newly combined entity.

No one believes that you should be overly friendly in a gruelling price negotiation. However, beyond this narrow context, a broader, more forward-looking agenda is at play and the opportunity for you to set the tone is one not to be missed.

Your reputation precedes you

Particularly true of serial acquirers, your reputation can become a millstone as counterparties 'see you coming'. It doesn't take long for this to become an issue. If – rightly or wrongly – you become known over a series of acquisitions as a company that doesn't care about the acquired employees or relationships with trade unions, this becomes something that needs focused management to address before the next deal begins. Such a reputation is not necessarily deserved – a company that has grown rapidly through acquisitions can quickly become known as aggressive and ruthless irrespective of their actual post-deal modus operandi.

Using your corporate affairs team (or closest equivalent) to keep tabs of your reputation, which may differ by geography or business unit, is important. Knowledge of how you will be perceived prima facie is critical to shaping your communications strategy and the way you brief your deal and integration teams, particularly when you are seeking to reset your reputation.

Be aware of the different channels used to formulate opinions. A communications team should cooperate with – or even be subordinated to – the integration team, to help define the key messages and script that will be delivered. Manage the rumour mill as well as every interaction with the counterparty. Use multiple channels – media, government officials, influencers, former employees of the target and advisors – to disseminate your key messages in a way that shapes the counterparty's perceptions.

Being cognisant of your reputation, and the impact that every interaction you and your representatives have on it, allows you to craft your message accordingly.

Project a credible view of the 'sunny uplands'

Change can be hard; some people will lose their jobs, and uncertainty and anxiety can destabilise integration and the wider business. People need to believe that the changes they are experiencing are happening for a greater purpose. Successfully creating the right kind of visualisation should be underpinned by a compelling picture of the future for all parties. All stakeholders have to believe that the radical changes that are likely to result from the acquisition or merger will be warranted on both an organisational level and, ultimately more importantly, personal level, to reduce the resistance to change (to the greatest extent possible).

While many who work in business, M&A and integration understand the concept of the change curve – the emotional journey experienced by those going through change – few consider the fact that, for those involved pre-close, the journey through the curve begins much earlier. Although the bulk of combined work and campaigning begins from the day the transaction closes – Day One – the groundwork begins prior to this, during the negotiations and detailed integration design. The driving force behind the change (new strategy, revenue increase, new markets, new technology development, etc.) must be very well understood and communicated throughout the pre-close activity to those working on – or even just aware of – the potential deal. By the time Day One arrives, the leadership of both companies should already have a solid understanding of – and hopefully support – the benefits and logic of the combination.

Beyond the analyst community's rationalisations and the media hype, a clear articulation of the vision, business case and definition of success is essential to raise sights beyond the immediate anxieties.

Make it personal

During the M&A and integration processes, there is one question on everyone's mind which overrides all other considerations – "What does this mean for me?" No individual or stakeholder is immune from this anxiety. Will I have a job? Who will I be working for? Where will I work? Will I enjoy working here, and what will it be like? What do my career prospects look like? Will my salary and benefits change?

Until these questions are satisfactorily addressed, resistance to the transaction and to the envisaged change will persist to a greater or lesser extent. Naturally, these cannot be answered fully prior to transaction close and, in reality, sometime into the integration execution phase. However, in the absence of clear messaging from the acquirer – or from the executives of companies involved in merger talks – the key stakeholders, in particular the employees, will fill a communication vacuum with their own perception of what is to ensue, fuelled by the ever-accelerating rumour mill.

Develop a stakeholder communication plan

While communication plans are in common use, preparing one early in the integration planning process is the mark of an experienced acquirer: one that covers not only Day One and the post-close messaging, but also the pre-close team concerns and expectations. Early preparation is also critical in managing the risk of pre-announcement deal leaks.

Like all communication plans, the key elements include:

- The **key messages** to be conveyed about the acquirer, the logic for the transaction, the vision for the combined entity and the process. These key messages will be adapted to match the phase of the transaction;

- The **key stakeholders** to whom the campaign is targeted – one's own employees, the target company employees, both sets of shareholders and boards, key suppliers and customers, local and national government officials, major joint venture partners, local communities and the like;

- An assessment of what each **stakeholder group's concerns** are likely to be at key points in the process;

- **Tailored messages** for each stakeholder group, which are a subset or version of the key messages;

- The **channels** through which each stakeholder group will be reached, including mainstream and social media, lobbyists or key influencers, specialist publications, consultants, direct meetings, letters, a special 'transaction' website, and the like.

People should be helped to not only feel like a part of the change, but like they are playing an active role in it. Often people are resistant towards change, not because they don't like the future, but because they feel a loss of certainty or control. If they can begin to feel a sense of ownership, they will not feel like something is being imposed upon them.

William Bridges' seminal change management work argues that people need to understand the Purpose, Picture (end-result), Plan, and Part (their personal role) in any major change management process. Integration communications are too often caught up in pushing the 'Picture' piece, meaning they are failing to address every concern. Efforts should be made to help push the more personal side of communications; what part will each person play in the integration, how do their own efforts contribute to the broader integration and the future of the company? Helping everyone to understand the different elements of the change in this way will allow them to feel a personal connection to it, generating the right kind of energy and support so that the final psychological piece can be unlocked (Managing Transitions: Making the Most of Change, 2003, William Bridges, Perseus Books).

Engage both parties

Recognising the need to build personal support for your deal pre-close can transform your thinking leading up to integration, and determine the ultimate outcome of the deal. Instead of focusing on the best way to compel or cajole the 'opposition' into making concessions and ensuring the best possible deal has been struck, the pre-deal process itself will start to create positive energy, confidence and support for the acquisition. Your team's perception is then reframed to become: how can you get the best deal possible for your company, without compromising your future ability to actually attain the benefits and synergies so desperately desired?

The answer is to mentally prepare both your team and 'the other side' for integration. If your team lacks strong conviction or confidence in your plan, you're on a highway to nowhere. Instead, everyone needs to get excited about and support the deal. They need to feel like both they and the company are on the way to bigger and better things.

Energy and support on both sides of the deal is vital. Paint a picture of the future vision of the company, and be honest in detailing the difficulties that will be faced. Most importantly, you need to connect on a more human level. Acquirers tend to define and communicate acquisition and integration from an organisational standpoint: how the *business* will benefit, what challenges and risks the *company* will face, what changes will impact *departments* or *teams*. While people should be interested in such things, you need to show that you understand how this plays out for them at a personal level: the need for increased workload, possible changes to roles or job losses, and the need to live with general uncertainty, at least for a while. Showing that you understand people's *personal* aspirations and highlighting opportunities to contribute and play a part in the future of a changing company, all the while being open and candid about the difficulties they will face, is the best way to gain credibility and generate momentum.

Certainty and credibility only comes with time, work and consistency. The integration team needs to be wholly confident going into a new environment and presenting themselves as bringers – and leaders – of widespread change. This confidence can only come about through a comprehensive vision of the integration objective and process, something that can only come from your detailed integration planning. Presenting this plan with confidence and displaying a real understanding of the workings of the organisation, as well as the difficulties and uncertainties that will be faced, will also encourage people to believe that the changes will happen and can be completed smoothly. While it is unlikely that everyone will whole-heartedly embrace the change, this will help people get past their inevitable scepticism and worry.

The view from our side: Visualise everything!

Feeling mentally prepared and comfortable in your surroundings is a daunting task for an integration team. With no prior knowledge of the company you'll be working in, one of the first things to do is to create a vivid visualisation of the company; what it will look and feel like once you're in there, drawing on data and insights from due diligence and putting them to work in an integration context.

Start with the basics: gather desktop data on the other company's organisational structure and their management team. Try to get a sense of their culture, what makes them tick, and their strategy.

This information can then be supplemented with direct research. Find out how the target company's products or services are sold, how they're positioned, and how customers perceive them. Working through the value chain can reveal valuable insights about what they produce, where they produce it, the investments they've recently made to underpin their strategy, and so on. Slowly an image of the company will emerge, and it becomes increasingly easy to visualise how to best lead the integration and change to come.

This view becomes more granular by looking at the company's component parts. By breaking this work into team structures, with Finance looking at Finance, HR at HR, etc., a far more complete and accurate view can be attained.

For example, instead of simply estimating the benefits of integrating two IT functions by looking at the historical results of similar initiatives elsewhere, you can conduct a deep dive into the operating model of the target IT department and what can be done with it, giving a more concrete idea of how many jobs will need to be cut, if any, who the key talent is and how the new operating model will look. What will the teams and reporting lines look like? What applications and methodologies will they be using? What development, testing and support approaches will be adopted? At an organisational level, define exactly how the new IT function will operate, while at a personal level, give your team a view of what it will feel like: Will this be a fun, interesting and challenging place to work, and should I commit to making this vision a reality?

Siemens PLM HR Integration Platform

Using best practices from other software companies, Siemens PLM created an online human resources integration platform that includes the operational and cultural aspects of an integration. This platform helps Siemens managers and employees prepare for and collaborate with its acquired companies.[2]

2: Siemens PLM Global HR M&A Integration. (2016). [video] Published by I. Morag.

Relevant information such as likely team costs, group location, and opportunities for deferred or shared hardware and software investments can then be shared across the deal team to ensure that no stone is left unturned.

Eventually, through this practice, everyone involved in the integration will be able to envisage the change, what they'll be doing, how they'll do it, and what could go wrong. People can use their knowledge to create and maintain a rolling list of hypotheses, adding and removing items as they uncover more information about the company and what other opportunities or threats exist.

Thorough research will build the confidence of the integration team. Such confidence cascades through the organisations even before you walk into the company on Day One. Equally, the employees of the target company are more likely to give the integration team the benefit of the doubt if they are introduced to a confident team with a clear vision of the future, and at least an initial plan of how to get there. Whether you're intending to merge your marketing channels to better serve your customers, to rebrand the company completely, or apply their engineering and technology capability to your portfolio, it is important to have a list of things that will have to be done in the short, medium and long-term. Consequently, the team running the integration can walk in on Day One and feel like they know exactly what they're doing, with this confidence cascading down through the company.

Generate asymmetric insight

Developing insight beyond that which is publicly available is the hardest part of building a detailed and credible picture of the target and of the challenge ahead. 'Asymmetric insight' uncovers new and unique perspectives on the organisation, new opportunities for value creation, and an enhanced understanding of the risks. Balancing opportunities against the potential risk is essential in any integration, and knowing that you've dedicated yourself to finding any potential opportunity to create more value or avoid more risk will ensure everyone is fully committed to the plan, knows what to expect and how to recover if anything goes wrong.

Talking directly to people is the most deceptively simple and overlooked way of generating such insight. It's easy to forget in the midst of a negotiation or due diligence period that talking to people with the relevant knowledge is both possible and potentially valuable. In our experience, temporarily hiring former (recent) employees from all relevant functions is one of the best ways to scrutinise and sense-check any existing hypotheses. This also serves the additional purpose of creating confidence within your integration teams that they are doing the right thing.

Other methods can be equally effective. Talking to others who have worked with the company can produce key insights: who are the best or most open-minded managers, how is their new strategy unfolding, and what are the opportunities for improvement? Key equipment suppliers are useful in helping you understand the physical constraints in the target's operations or even IT infrastructure.

Enormous dividends can be yielded from these activities, such as uncovering important individuals within the company who'll need to support the integration or potential value creation opportunities. Broader benefits are also likely, such as gaining a more detailed view of any potential synergies or risks you believe may exist, or of which you may not have been aware.

Ultimately, the main reason to embark on such work is to make sure that your integration team shares a solid picture of the company and gains confidence in their plans. This can help finalise your list of hypotheses about what will be done post-close and ensure everyone knows – and is comfortable with – their role.

Work out what is not negotiable

Integrations are full of compromise, but there are some principles and values that make a company what it is. If these are broken, the identity of the company and the factors that generate a competitive advantage can unravel. As discussed in Chapter 1, never go through an integration without a clear view of what is sacrosanct: recognising these principles can help to create a sense of clarity about the end goal. Failing to do so can jeopardise your own organisation, disrupting and demotivating those within your business and derailing the entire process.

A clear understanding of your own organisational 'red lines' can also help you value the target accurately, and even determine whether the deal is right after all. For example, Xstrata were wedded to their organisational constructs – in particular, the devolution of authority, having no central functions, a very small corporate head office and high personal accountability. These were the guiding principles around which there was no negotiation. If implementing these principles in the target company would cause significantly more disruption, this could lead to an adjustment of the valuation or a change in the integration strategy; if this cultural change were seen to be too dramatic or difficult, halting the deal itself may be the only choice.

Isolating these immutable values and principles is harder than people anticipate. While numerous companies would be unrecognisable without some particular cultural traits, recognising which ones truly define the company's DNA and make it successful over the long-term often is only possible through continual discussion, brainstorming and workshopping. You and your key management need to agree on what is essential for the combined company, prior to defining your negotiating position and integration plan.

An agreed merger can sometimes be the exception to the

rule of ensuring your guiding principles survive into the new, combined organisation. In this context, a significant amount of joint work is required by the new executive team to determine which components of each company's DNA are desirable for long-term success and why. Once this is done, a new set of immutable values and principles can be drawn up and used to guide the integration and restructuring of the business. This should be done before Day One.

Build the future together

Takeda and Millennium Pharmaceuticals: prioritizing trust and transparency

Soon after a transaction seemed possible between Japanese pharmaceutical giant Takeda and US biotechnology company Millennium Pharmaceuticals, the conversation turned to their cultural compatibility. The acquisition process involved multiple conversations on common values, functional integration and how to communicate transparently to build trust. To support their agreed joint cultural DNA, processes were developed with input from both sides to maintain strong innovation and collaboration.[3]

In an agreed transaction, one of the best ways to build understanding and engagement from leaders of both

---

3: https://www.fticonsulting.com/~/media/Files/us-files/insights/journal-articles/biotech-and-big-pharma-keys-to-a-successful-m-and-a.pdf organisations is to have them work closely to build the future 'target operating model' for the combined business. Wherever possible, bring the management teams from both sides of the deal together and workshop your collective thinking around strategy, proposition, branding, core capabilities, structure, culture and more. Doing this prior to the close of the transaction can of course present difficulties relating to the exchange of sensitive information. Processes must be put in place to ensure that commercially sensitive and confidential information – mostly around intellectual property and and customer data – is protected and excluded from such joint discussions, and any analysis is conducted confidentially (e.g. by using a 'clean room' administered by a third party). Where such sensitive work requires data from both sides, this third party can generate aggregate or sanitised analyses and recommendations based on the confidential information they are entrusted with by each company. The need for confidentiality does not restrict your ability to bring the management teams together to discuss and develop the future vision and plan.

A better sense of the future is also the foundation upon which to build momentum, creating a platform from which to quickly propagate a *shared* vision of the future, beginning in earnest on Day One.

KEY CONCEPTS:

1. Test your mental models about the target company, its people and the way it operates by actively seeking disconfirming evidence.

2. Manage your public and private image throughout the pre-close activities to limit the potential for undue resistance to your integration plans:

   a. Send the right messages to the other side's deal team to prepare the ground for change;

   b. Create a clear and credible vision of the future combined entity and the inherent logic of the transaction. Project these at every opportunity to all relevant stakeholders using a detailed stakeholder communications plan.

3. Generate a detailed picture of the target company and share this with everyone involved in the integration.

4. Maintain a rolling list of hypotheses about the actions to be taken after Day One, refining the list as new data emerges. Share this list with all those involved in the integration.

5. Be clear about which principles guiding your organisation are immutable and embed these into your integration design and plan.

6. As soon as possible before or after Day One, bring both sides together to build a joint vision of the future with the target company executives and integration teams.

Chapter 3:
CHANGE IS EXPECTED – DON'T DISAPPOINT

"Cleverness has never been associated with long delays."
SUN TZU – THE ART OF WAR

"Having seen acquirers behave like bulls in china shops, Paul knew it was important for him and his team to listen and learn before acting. With that in mind, the integration team was given strict instructions not to dive into their integration plans the minute the deal was concluded. Messaging around Day One was muted and cautious, the only clear message being given was that 'nothing will change for now' – sensitive, respectful and open to ideas. The four-week 'discovery' phase that ensued was very helpful in confirming that they knew enough about Lidare and their ways of working, building relationships, and making sure that the integration plans they had sketched out were further developed with realism and accuracy.

And yet despite this, once integration began in earnest on Day 31 with new branding and signs, everyone was suddenly up in arms. Paul simply didn't understand: why couldn't Lidare's team recognise, let alone appreciate, Paul's intense efforts to make sure Day One was as close as it could be to business as usual?"

Congratulations! You now own the company. To paraphrase the proverbial dog that caught the car – "Now what?"

On completion of a deal, an acquirer is faced with a series of choices, the first and most obvious of which is – "how quickly do I bring about the changes I have planned for the acquired organisation?"

Speed of change is a hotly debated topic amongst senior executives and, in particular, integration managers. Some argue for a more tactful and sensitive approach, designed to allow the newly acquired employees to overcome their anxieties and perceived loss of independence. This will result in a smoother, more collaborative integration down the line. Further, the advocates of a slower approach make the point that patience affords them more time to better understand the organisation they have acquired, thereby leading to better integration plans and fewer mistakes.

When the acquired entity is to be integrated or changed significantly, this approach – while often well intended – is usually counterproductive. Furthermore, it may be seen as disingenuous unless your communications are exceptionally well managed.

While each integration clearly has its own idiosyncrasies, and some may require a more 'gentle' approach, our strong bias is to move as quickly as possible once the transaction has closed. In fact, you need to move even more quickly than you yourself might want (Hooper, 2018).[1]

Why? There are numerous reasons for speed, the most important of which is that you have been afforded a licence for change. An acquisition brings with it an expectation that things will not be the same. You have a window of opportunity during which, although they may not fully agree with or like the changes you are planning, people from both organisations – yours and the target's – are mentally and emotionally prepared for radical change. The same applies to all other stakeholders, including customers, communities, trade unions, governments, suppliers and the like. Disappointing them by dragging your feet erodes momentum and wastes a unique moment in which you have permission to drastically transform the business. Worse still, if change has been minimal or non-existent for six months or more post-close, organisations and relationships re-ossify, the 'compelling need' for integration recedes from people's minds, and change becomes exponentially more difficult to bring about. The window closes.

So, rip off the bandage as quickly as possible to minimise the long-term pain.

1: Hooper, T. (2018). Enterprise Drives Innovation Through M&A. [online] Forbes.com. Available at: https://www.forbes.com/sites/mergermarket/2018/09/20/enterprise-drives-innovation-through-ma/ [Accessed 25 Jan. 2019].

Why else does speed make sense?

Uncertainty is in itself an unhelpful state to prolong. Productivity plummets, rumour mills proliferate and the organisation loses focus and, often, key people. There is no substitute for action as a means of providing the organisation with a sense of momentum towards the stated goal. As painful as this transformation may be, it is preferable to stagnation and continued uncertainty. Momentum in and of itself will undoubtedly reduce resistance.

Don't forget: a fast, efficient integration will deliver the planned synergies more quickly, realising value and settling the organisation back into 'business as usual' in short order. Sooner started, sooner finished.

For serial acquirers, especially in rapidly consolidating industries, completing the integration quickly also enables them to get back on the acquisition path so as not to miss the next important opportunity.

Finally, the sooner the integration team members are finished, the sooner they can get back to their day jobs. Integration can also be very disruptive for the core business, and a speedy integration minimises this period of disturbance.

This does not mean however that diving in blindly is the right move. As Benjamin Franklin purportedly warned, "haste makes great waste". Mistakes are inevitable in a speedy integration. This is where extensive preparation pre-close comes in. The better prepared you and your team are as the transaction closing approaches, the more you will know and the fewer mistakes you will make. Prioritising what's important for value creation, the target operating model, risk mitigation and 'must do' activities, will mean you'll know what activities to defer until later. Don't sweat the small stuff – integration is too complex and intense to try to do everything perfectly at once.

In all, why wait? You bought the company to achieve a set of goals, and when these goals necessitate integration, you should start as early as possible.

Show your hand

There is no better time to signal momentum, professionalism and intent than at the series of events we characterise as 'Day One'.

The Day One period should set the tone for the oncoming integration, reveal your culture and management style to the acquired business and outline the changes that are to come; while simultaneously asserting your team's authority and credibility. The first and most important benefit is clear – it gets the ball rolling. Integration tends to rely on momentum, without which the process may founder. Moreover, sharing your plans early reduces debilitating uncertainty, while laying out your stall will help employees decide whether to enthusiastically sign up, or instead consider their exit.

Your very first contact post-close should reflect these aims and signal your desire to take charge, giving the distinct impression you know exactly what you are doing. Like all other aspects of communication, the intent is to build trust and credibility in your vision, your plans and your ability to get there; Day One is the first step in this effort. People *want* to be led through potential turbulence and uncertainty and are more likely to drop their resistance if your story is compelling and your prowess clear.

Vague plans, high-level assurances and platitudes, or signalling too much inclusiveness will bring about the opposite outcome to what is intended. Uncertainty and resistance will increase with an escalating potential for disruptive forces. Mark Sirower reinforces this in his book, "The Synergy Trap"[2], in which he highlights the correlation between the level of detail you provide about your post-close plans in your deal announcement and the immediate change in share price of the company. If a CEO stands up and talks clearly about the plan, what they want to achieve and how they'll get there, the share price tends to increase – "these people seem to know that they're doing and why". When the

---

2: *The Synergy Trap: How Companies Lose the Acquisition Game*, Mark Sirower, Simon & Schuster, 1997, 2008.

CEO fails to provide sufficient detail or suggests a plan is yet to be formulated, the share price tends to fall – "they really have no idea, do they?" Worst of all is the famous line still heard far too often: "Don't worry, nothing will change". This is very rarely the true long-term intention and is therefore the best way to lose credibility and trust once the inevitable change does begin.

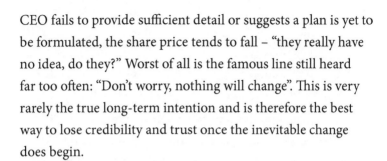

Pay attention to what's being said about you and around you

The merger of Austrian company bwin and UK's PartyGaming was a significant deal within each company's home country. Both were major players in their local markets and therefore attracted the attention of the local press. Though the deal was progressing successfully, the press portrayed PartyGaming as a foreign company taking over a national treasure, repeatedly criticising the deal. As bwin employees followed the news coverage, morale worsened and staff flight increased. This was despite a considerable amount of positive internal communications taking place.

It is not only employees who need reassurance; what you say to the market is also key. For example, when Quaker Oats acquired Snapple in 1994, Quaker Chairman and CEO William Smithburg stated that the acquisition "brings together the marketing muscle and growth potential of two of the great brands in an incredibly health-conscious America". Nice words, but unfortunately, they were not enough to convince the stock market. Quaker paid no premium for Snapple but lost 10% of its market value – almost $500 million – the moment this announcement was released.

Conversely, when announcing the acquisition of Dresden Papier in March 2013, the CEO of Glatfelter, a mid-cap manufacturing firm with revenues at the time of $1.7 billion, stated:

> "*The acquisition of Dresden Papier will add another industry-leading non-wovens product line to our Composite Fibers business, and broaden our relationship with leading producers of consumer and industrial products. Despite the ongoing economic challenges in parts of Europe, we believe the global nonwoven wallpaper business will continue to grow at a compound annual growth rate of at least 10%. This acquisition will also provide additional operational leverage and growth opportunities for Glatfelter globally, particularly in large markets such as Russia and China, and other developing markets in eastern Europe and Asia.*"

Their share price immediately increased by a staggering 28% – and went on to rise by a further 29% in the coming months as integration progressed.

In this example, Glatfelter gave a simple, logical statement focused on the rationale, context and benefits of the deal; backed up by specifics and targets. They answered the two basic questions the investment community always ask: How specifically is this deal going to benefit your firm, and how are you going to achieve it?

Being clear and specific is the right approach, but it only works if you've done your homework. Ensuring your Day One activities fulfil these aims requires intensive preparation and careful consideration.

Get your story straight!

Although a day or two of intensive communication is the best way to launch an integration process, Day One is not a single day – it encompasses a series of communication and other activities involving all stakeholders which may cover two or more weeks.

Day One: Preparation

It is worth repeating that your ability to gain support depends on how clear you are about why you bought the business and your vision for the future. You need to articulate both in a way that makes them compelling and exciting. Being clear on these fundamentals will form an essential part of Day One aimed at engaging those who subscribe to the company's vision and ethos early. A critical part of this is knowing what the future will look like – what role will the company and its people play, what the integration will look like, and what benefits can be delivered to all stakeholders.

Day One Checklist

✔ Develop a consistent message to all stakeholders (Communications Plan)

✔ Prepare the story and the presentations

✔ Decide on the top management team

✔ Make symbolic changes

✔ Check logistics – and check them again

Calamity can be avoided by ensuring the message is consistent and fully understood by each manager involved in sharing the vision. This means preparing the right message, to be delivered in the same tone and style, while fully preparing for any eventuality in Q&A sessions, no matter how challenging. It's embarrassing to say the least, if the CEOs of the acquiring and acquired company have disjointed and disharmonious messages. More harmful still, inconsistent messages will create the impression that the new plan is not set in stone, or that discord at the executive level will be a sign of things to come. Even powerhouses like Disney and ABC are not immune to messaging mistakes. When announcing their merger in 1996, Disney and ABC released statements that highlighted a lack of coordination and understanding of the synergies to be achieved from the relationship, forcing key external stakeholders to question the potential success of the deal.

One of the very few universal rules of post-acquisition

integration remains: the top executive team running the integrated company should be agreed before Day One. To the extent that it's possible, select (and make conditional offers to) at least the top layer of new executives before transaction close. Getting the new management team (which will likely include people from the acquired company) on board is an incredibly powerful signal – it shows from the outset that real change will be made and that the acquired company leadership is already on board with the vision of the future. Most importantly, it signals momentum.

Other symbolic 'high-visibility' actions signalling a serious intent to change should be identified and taken if full integration is intended – rebranding, new leadership, relocation being common examples. These can act as powerful agents of change. A tsunami of activity of this sort will remove anchors to the old company (things that create inertia or prolong nostalgia for the past), and sweep employees in the desired direction towards the future.

Xstrata's Symbolic Gesture – The Power of a Quick Office Move

Symbolic changes can be big or small, and can do much to help people adjust to change. When Xstrata acquired Falconbridge in Canada in a $20bn transaction, they quickly realised the existing office block was not connected to 'The Path', an underground maze of tunnels in Toronto connecting buildings and protecting

commuting staff from the ravages of Toronto's harsh winters.
Xstrata were able to create goodwill by quickly moving to new
downtown offices, on 'The Path'. In any scenario, an office move
is strongly symbolic of change and of leaving the past behind and
should be strongly considered where possible.

The merger of two IT gaming companies to create a new
brand offers a powerful example. On the Friday before
Day One, employees left the building as normal. When
they returned on Monday, the office had been completely
renovated to reflect the new branding: walls had been
repainted, new signs erected, new mouse pads were
distributed, screensavers were changed, log-in details and
email domains were updated, new business cards were
printed, and employees were migrated to the relevant
software and databases. Symbols of the old company had been
expunged, replaced by the new logos and branding. While
at first appearing extreme, these actions provide finality,
signal momentum, generate excitement and enthusiasm
for the future, and reduce resistance to the 'new'. Naturally,
immediate branding changes are not sufficient to deliver
the value envisaged in the acquisition but are important in
creating a fertile ground for change.

This approach may be seen as going against change
management best practice which states that such actions
should not ignore, or worse still, intentionally obliterate the

past. As William Bridges (Bridges, 2003)[2] states, people need time to 'let go' of the past before they can embrace the future. Yes and yes – the two approaches are complementary if done well. Celebrate and memorialise the achievements of the past company, openly talk about how the new future is building on the successes of the old, adding new layers to the journey – but if you do it quickly, and present a strong clear plan, people will be more prepared to move on.

Remember, the message is not all about you, nor should it be all about them. It is about your future journey together. Too many acquirers focus their Day One presentation on themselves – how great a company we are (and therefore how lucky you should feel to have been picked to join us), how good a company we are to work within (and therefore by comparison how poor yours was, only yesterday), and the benefits and financial returns the company will reap (at your expense). Like any first date, spending the evening talking yourself up and showing no interest in the other party generally backfires.

Changes to the identity of the business must be accompanied by preparation for your communications with external groups. For example, customer-facing employees need training and collateral soon after Day One to enable them to represent the new company with confidence and enthusiasm. Corporate

---

2: Bridges, W. (2003). Managing transitions. London: Nicholas Brealey Publishing.

affairs executives require briefing on the company's position on key issues of relevance to local and national governments, as well as to community leaders so they can present a compelling picture of the new organisation. These changes cannot be made until Day One itself, but it is important to think through every touch point with stakeholders such as customers (not only sales teams but also people from post-sales support, finance, logistics etc.). Having identified these points of interaction, key messages and materials should be prepared in advance. These could be as simple as a 'rules of engagement' guide giving different internal teams the basic information needed to carry on with their role but should also include (their own personalised version of) the vision and benefits of the deal, and how this will improve things for them and their group. This set of activities must be replicated for each major stakeholder group. For example, letters to key government officials, community leaders, suppliers, customers and other relevant groups must be dispatched on Day One to follow the ones sent when the transaction became public. These letters should describe in brief the vision as it relates to those stakeholders and, importantly, when they can expect to hear directly from a company representative.

Finally, Day One logistics need to be given due consideration. Every part of the Day One agenda (example below) should be intricately planned, from the location to groupings for breakout sessions to social events. Make sure you stress-test the plan for vulnerabilities and risks, using 'Red Team review' or similar approaches, consider unanticipated events and prepare contingency plans in case something goes wrong. What if the CEO can't get to the meeting? What if the projector stops working? Transportation problems? While perhaps sounding trivial, the unintended consequence of a minor problem can be a widespread reputation for disorganisation, lack of attention to detail or even a lack of interest in 'getting it right on your first day'. Big issues, but simply avoided with a bit of advance planning.

Day One: Example agenda

By and large, the purpose, and therefore agenda, for Day One tends to be similar across industries, deal sizes and aims, although some elements may be scaled up or down and tweaked accordingly. The devil is in the detail – the venue should be specially selected, logistics for arrivals carefully calibrated, the environment should be made friendly and neutral, and the events themselves thoroughly planned. All of these elements require careful preparation, and this section should at least give food for thought when designing such an event.

As previously mentioned, it's often helpful to consider Day One as lasting more than one day. Typically, it comprises a major event for the senior management of both the acquired and acquiring companies, as well as workshops and roadshows for employees, and other similar events with the relevant stakeholders.

The template below provides a generic Day One agenda:

Sample Day One Agenda

	Pre-Day One	Day One	Day 2 and beyond
Communications		Webcast and slides to be distributed following morning presentation	
09h00	Signage and Security Arrivals and Final Preparations	**Exec 1-on-1 meetings to confirm new appointments**	Functional Breakout Groups: (Finance,IT,HR,Treasury, Corporate Affairs, Sustainable Development, Treasury, Insurance, Marketing, Logistics, etc.) 1. Introduction to Function 2. Integration Plan — Government Stakeholder Meeting(s) Site visits
11h30		**EXCO Meeting**	
12h00			
13h30		**Registration** Guest list, badges and gifts to be arranged	
14h00		**Launch:** 1. Head of Integration – Welcome 2. CEO – Introduction to the Company, deal rationale, new top structure, asset summary 3. CFO – Financial highlights of new Combined Company; governance 4. Corporate Affairs – Corporate History / Investor perspective 5. Head of Integration – Integration Process, Q&A session	
15h00			
16h00		**[Transfer to venues] Afternoon Tea**	
16h30	Team Briefing	**Business Unit (BU) Breakout Groups:** Brief introduction to each BU Team leaders to prepare: 1. Asset overview (in conjunction with Target Company counterparts) 2. Integration Plan — **Exec 1-on-1s continued as required**	Site/Functional planning and visits begin — Potential Government Stakeholder Meeting(s): CEO/CFO/COO/Corporate Affairs
17h00			
18h00 for 18h30		**All attendees at Day One – BBQ (offsite)** (CEO: Short word and thank previous execs)	**Integration Team Meeting**

Senior management event

For larger deals, this should be held in a venue in the town or city most important to the acquired company, but for smaller deals it is likely to be held at or near the acquiring company's office. The aim should be to provide as much information as possible about the deal and the road ahead, start to build relationships, display your organisation's culture and instil trust and credibility. Each part of this event should be tailored to ensure this happens.

Whom to Invite

The simple answer would be 'the Top 100' from each company. Of course, the number of people depends on the size of the acquired organisation. The participants should have corresponding business units and functions represented from both sides of the deal. If possible – at least at the morning session – there should be a larger number of representatives from the acquired company, but keeping in mind that it is important not to 'swamp' the acquired employees with a larger number of your own people. The intent is for the senior members of the two companies to hear the vision of the combined company and get to know each other both socially and in the work context through the initial workshops.

The morning session

The morning session is crucial in setting the tone and relaying enough information to ease people's anxieties about the deal, their personal future and their new bosses. To start, the acquiring executive team – starting with the CEO – should deliver a presentation welcoming the new employees into the company. No promises are made at this point on who will be there in the future, but the story should lay down your company's history, what you are trying to achieve, and how the acquisition fits into that vision, as well as basic details on the values of your company and how people are expected to behave.

The new team chosen to run the integrated company – who will be sitting at the table with the acquiring executive team – should then be introduced. This sends a powerful signal, showing that real change is already being made, and that people from their legacy organisation are already on board. The next topic is typically the integration itself – how it will work, the key steps and possible risks, what to expect, what you are hoping to achieve, and – crucially – the timetable. Setting out the milestones at which staff will hear about key developments, especially their futures, is an important part of managing anxieties. Again, this should make people more receptive and willing to listen to you, so instead of trying to pander to them and promising stability you can cement your credibility and integrity with a very clear plan. Moreover, people will recognise the intent to act as quickly as possible, helping people realise and accept that change is inevitable. Be open with your view of the issues and challenges you are likely to face together. Nothing builds that trust and credibility like a balanced perspective.

'Setting out your stall' in such a manner informs people of the future and helps them make a conscious choice about whether or not they want to be there. People should be given enough to know the behavioural expectations (values, principles, culture), what it will take to succeed in the new organisation and how things will change, allowing them to begin making an informed decision about how they wish to approach integration and their role in it. 'Force' management and staff to consider, as quickly as possible, their commitment to the future, rather than allowing them to adopt a 'wait and watch' mindset.

Afternoon sessions

The next stage is intended to help people get to know who they'll be working with and what they are like. More helpfully still, it should begin to dispel any lingering misconceptions about the people on the other side of the deal. We recommend breaking into pre-determined groups of people who will be working closely with one another, generally by business unit or function. The ice can then be broken by getting teams to present how things are currently done in their particular business unit or function, what their goals are, what has been achieved and what their future plans are. This lets each team start off on a familiar footing, providing an opportunity to showcase their work, while presenting their views of how they should integrate or be integrated into the combined entity.

This introductory session should allow groups to discuss their concerns about the integration process, the differences between the companies as they see them and other issues which may present obstacles to a successful integration. With the acquiring team, there is an opportunity here to properly set the tone for future interaction – do you act as a peer or something more authoritative? The instinct here is often to make people comfortable, but in truth the acquirer needs to strike the correct balance between peer and conqueror. Naturally, in something resembling a merger, the style should probably be more egalitarian, while in a takeover the acquiring party sets the basic rules, without ignoring the values or views presented by the target company. If you can successfully strike the right tone you can eliminate the notion of 'winners vs. losers', by painting a positive view of the combined business unit or function and showing openness and a desire to succeed together.

For example, when Xstrata acquired Falconbridge, the Xstrata executive team recognised that the business was entering a phase of significant project-based development, but that Xstrata did not have the requisite project management and engineering capabilities to support its plans. Falconbridge, on the other hand, had developed numerous large capital projects over the years and Xstrata management were keen to retain this capability within the combined entity. With this in mind, Xstrata appointed Falconbridge's former head of projects as the CEO of one of its operating units. Xstrata then incorporated Falconbridge's strengths and capabilities into that unit, with a view to making this knowhow available to the entire combined company.

Integration will be delivered by both business units and functional teams using people from both sides of the transaction. Unless fully absorbed elsewhere, the leader of the acquired unit is usually selected from the acquiring company. However sometimes a senior executive from the acquired business can be chosen to strike a balance between continuity and change.

Social Event

The final event is social, designed to get individuals to meet each other in a relaxed, non-business setting, break down barriers and encourage everyone to see each other as individuals with similar interests, anxieties and ambitions. Of course, questions about the future should be invited, but equally everyone should be free to talk about their personal interests. Consequently, we'd suggest seating plans are carefully designed to place relevant people from each company next to each other.

Dinner can culminate with the CEO of the acquiring company making a speech, focusing again on the culture of the company and the vision. This should then be followed by another important opportunity to let acquired company representatives ask questions. By this point significant information – formal and informal – would have been shared on the culture of the company and the operating specifics to enable valuable questions to surface. Being prepared through Q&As will help ensure confident and consistent answers, providing clarity about the vision and encouraging a positive outlook on the future.

Stakeholder meetings

The remainder of the Day One activities (typically starting on the following day) should be dedicated to meeting other groups within the combined company. How many meetings and with whom will vary from case to case, but the remaining employees of the acquired company should always be the first on your list. Presentations and meetings should be held at each group's own place of work, including operating sites where relevant, and the same presentation given to the executives in the morning session of Day One should be delivered to employees over the week or two following the transaction close.

Presentations should be led by the most credible and trusted source for each group, which is likely to be the acquiring company's relevant line or functional manager. Again, the focus here is to clearly articulate the short and longer-term implications of the transaction, inspiring confidence while easing uncertainty and anxiety.

Employee meetings should be followed by further Q&A sessions. While many questions are likely to be specific to the function or operating unit, the underlying anxiety is almost universally related to the 'what does this mean for me' question. If firm plans exist to restructure a department or unit, potentially resulting in redundancies, do not deliver an evasive or disingenuous message. It is far better in the long run to provide a straight-up view of what is being considered or what may be necessary for the future success of the business. Give clear deadlines by which any final decisions or plan will be available. False assurances that are reversed or broken later will only come back to haunt you – and your efforts to deliver deal benefits – further down the line.

Finally, it will be necessary to meet with other stakeholders beyond managers and employees. This could include the local mayor, trade union leaders, the central government, and selected local and national media channels. These stakeholders, the key messages pertaining the each of them and the channels through which you will reach them must be identified prior to the transaction close in the stakeholder communications plan (Chapter 2), but refined in collaboration with the acquired company's management and corporate affairs staff.

Background activities

Of course, talking to people isn't all you should do on Day One. You also now own the new company, with all its assets, people, obligations and activites. You need to take control immediately – ensure the cash and – at least as important – systems are secure, key processes are running smoothly and your mobile and digital assets, in particular, do not sprout legs and leave your premises.

Individual Points of Failure

In smaller businesses, single points of dependency and failure are not uncommon, and can be very risky. One newly-acquired company saw the acquired CEO depart on Day One, followed six months later by his personal secretary. Only then did the acquirer become aware (the hard way) that the secretary was the only individual in the unit with authority to operate the unit's bank account. Such possibilities, often considered too detailed for Day One, should be anticipated during detailed planning.

The first thing to do is ensure the business is operating safely and poses no risk to employees or others. A close second is to then secure your physical and digital assets. If employees are leaving, make sure their access to the premises and systems are revoked and email accounts are blocked. Any other actions essential to business security and operations must be prioritised and tracked to rapid completion. In the most extreme of cases, resentful former employees could use their access to sensitive commercial information or vital functions to launch a malicious attack against the company, including physical vandalism of the office or operating site. While these incidents are rare, it is prudent to prepare yourself for any eventuality.

Below are examples of 'must-do' activities which your integration teams will have identified during detailed integration planning and which are now activated. They include:

- Review all security arrangements. Secure access to the building, and ensure your team has access cards/keys;

- Cancel all departing employee and dormant access cards;

- Cancel all departing employee credit and other charge cards (e.g. fuel cards);

- Recover mobile assets from departing employees;

- Freeze recruitment of employees and consultants without specific approval by the Integration Director;

- Secure mobile assets, such as cars and equipment, including offsite equipment;

- Review and, where necessary, revise all major purchase orders and expenditure commitments;

- Take control of all bank accounts, review signature policies and amend accordingly;

- Prepare interim living and office arrangements and telephone, computer and other infrastructure for those members of your team who will be temporarily placed at the acquired sites during the integration;

- Replace signage, screen-savers, telephone greetings, e-mail addresses, security passes, passwords and publications with the combined company's branding and materials;

• Integrate e-mail servers and homogenise e-mail addresses as appropriate;

• Remove all spending and other decision authority limits throughout the acquired organisation and immediately replace with the combined entity's authority levels.

Occasionally, acquiring companies impose stricter spending limits on the newly-acquired entity for a period of time before relaxing them once the organisation has bedded down. Where appropriate, any new expense procedures and approval processes must be immediately imposed and communicated to all parties.

In an unconventional approach, some experienced acquirers appoint all their integration team leaders – who are largely their own employees – as Interim Managers, wholly and fully responsible for the day-to-day operations of their respective functions and business units, even if a counterpart already exists within the acquired company. This step is taken to ensure control is secured on Day One and critical new procedures and approaches are immediately installed. The Interim Managers hand over control to the permanent functional or business unit heads once they have been confirmed in their role and each operation is in steady state. This period of interim management can vary from a few days to many months, depending on the complexity of the integration for that function or business unit and the availability of a suitable permanent manager. Even where not adopted wholesale, many acquirers appoint an interim Finance Director drawn from their own team. As 'their man' (or woman) in the new acquisition, they can embed mandatory finance and reporting processes, and ensure financial visibility and control.

Furthermore, if there is the potential for a single point of failure (i.e. a key employee in sales or R&D, or a server on which the company's software products are hosted), this is a significant vulnerability that needs to be identified and addressed as quickly as possible.

While your due diligence may be thorough and comprehensive, there are bound to be aspects of the 'must-do' agenda not identified pre-close, and which will come to light as you enter the front door as an owner. Ensure that you keep a live list of these activities – and if they represent risk, develop and activate mitigation plans immediately. Each Integration Team Leader and the Integration Director should be responsible for updating the Day One 'must-do' list and the risk analysis.

KEY CONCEPTS:

1. Move as quickly as possible to maintain momentum, exploit the licence for change and get the business onto a steady-state footing as soon as possible.

2. If a full integration is not appropriate, think carefully about where and how you may want to change, combine or align different aspects of the business: what will deliver maximum deal benefit?

3. Use the Day One series of events to set out your stall early with all stakeholders and to signal change:

   a. Announce the top team to run the combined company;

   b. Articulate your vision and key elements of your strategy for the new entity;

   c. Share any firm plans and avoid commitments which, if broken, would undermine your credibility later on;

   d. Provide details of the integration process, including key milestones;

   e. Start with top management and move quickly to the remaining employees and other key stakeholders.

4. Prepare detailed 'must-do' lists for the integration to ensure you take control on Day One and minimise the risk of disruption.

Chapter 4:
BUILD AND SUSTAIN MOMENTUM

"Tread water for long enough and you will eventually sink."
ANON

"Day One had been hailed as an unqualified success. Listening to the advice from John and his communications team, Quintado had put their best foot forward, setting the right tone for the future, outlining the vision and, most importantly, ensuring full and open dialogue to ensure the Lidare team heard, understood, believed and supported their plans. Everyone they had hoped to keep – even Jason from R&D – had agreed to the retention bonus, and performance over the first couple of months suggested that integration targets and the budget would be met. While there was a lot of work still to do, Paul worked hard to get people back to their normal day roles, leaving the programme team to focus on integration. He was even able to disband the communications workstream early. John's concerns around 'the change curve' and other consultancy mumbo jumbo simply didn't reflect Paul's gut feel and what he heard from his top team.

Now, six months later, with an almost palpable sense of integration stalling, Paul was beginning to think that perhaps

*discontinuing all integration-related communications hadn't
been the right move. His early mantra of 'business as usual'
was supported by every textbook on integration as well as his
own experience in previous (admittedly smaller) deals, but in
hindsight it clearly wasn't working here. Maybe it was time to
bring John back in, eat some humble pie, and get his view on
what was really going on…"*

Momentum is the lifeblood of any successful organisation. It
is also the most powerful of change agents and this is nowhere
more applicable and essential than in integration. Success
in creating momentum – literally from Day One – and
sustaining it through integration determines whether your
deal is destined for success.

Think of momentum as the minimum airflow required
under the wings of an aeroplane to keep it airborne. A loss
of forward motion at any point along the way simply results
in a crash – or at least a stall, from which only the most
experienced pilot can recover.

Momentum is nothing less than a product of good leadership
and begins with actions.

Oh yes, and did we say "move quickly, more quickly than
you're comfortable doing"? Everyone should feel a sense of
urgency; if things are feeling too comfortable you're probably
moving too slowly.

Clarity and leadership

In Chapter 3, we stressed the importance of appointing the top one or two tiers of management on Day One. This signals action, it communicates intent and it removes a significant uncertainty from the minds of the employees.

A second ingredient is the clear message about who's in charge. This relates to the appointment of the top team, but also the ability to strike the right balance between inclusiveness and decisiveness. Too much consultation can lead to stasis. On the other hand, heavy handedness will alienate large swathes of your organisation, increasing their resistance to the changes you wish to make and, eventually, destroying that vital momentum. Which end of the tightrope you chose to favour will depend on many factors including culture, both organisational and geographic. Some cultures are more responsive to clear directives and authority, while others react positively to being extensively consulted. Irrespective of which culture you find yourself in and the resulting approach you adopt to get to the right answer, there should be no doubt as to who's in charge. Naturally, this is easier to achieve – and is more legitimate – in a straight acquisition.

Clarity is further supported by quickly communicating cascaded authority limits through the organisation, most usually achieved with a register of Delegated Authorities, which governs, for example, purchase approvals, external communications, capital investment, ad hoc commercial decisions and other key concerns.

Pursue early victories

Nothing creates positive momentum like success itself. Everyone wants to be part of a winning team and the discipline to communicate the successful attainment of milestones – no matter how small or seemingly trivial – is vital in demonstrating momentum.

Set and communicate long-term and achievable short-term goals. Review them regularly, let people know what's being targeted in the next period (week, month, quarter) and trumpet their achievement.

Each integration team's plan should include a specific list of potential early victories – the low-hanging fruit that is both symbolic and potentially meaningful in bringing about change towards the new organisation and culture. Such quick wins can include those symbolic changes to the company identity discussed in Chapter 3 (signage, logos, names, stationery, business cards, etc.), and other decisive actions that signpost the new direction of the business such as cancellation of major capital that does not fit into the strategy of the combined entity, or renegotiation of key supply agreements based on best practice in each organisation.

Naturally, communicating these 'victories' as they appear is central to creating a sense of momentum. It can be helpful to go even further in these early stages when some may still doubt your ability to deliver on the promises you made on Day One; actively celebrate these quick wins, holding small events to recognise the progress, congratulate the team, and reinforce the message that this progress is genuinely important to you, the business, and them. This element of communication will be further discussed in Chapter 7.

Manage resistance

As we've highlighted, resistance comes in many forms, some obvious, some more insidious. Irrespective of the guise, resistance cannot be ignored lest it snowball into an irreversible, ossifying force. Within six months of Kraft's acquisition of Cadbury, 120 of the 165 Cadbury senior staff members left the company (BBC News, 2010).[1]

The precise nature of your response is, naturally, related to the source, nature and cause of resistance. Occasionally, a simple explanation of the process and expected milestones can put minds at ease. In other instances, the anxiety which leads to resistance is more deep-seated and requires an understanding of the root causes. Beyond this, a threat to vested interests can result in less obvious sources and forms of resistance.

1: BBC News. (2010). Staff quit Cadbury after takeover. [online] Available at: https://www.bbc.co.uk/news/uk-england-birmingham-10789983 [Accessed 25 Jan. 2019].

Remember, resistance to change is a common reaction to a sense of loss of *personal control*, and an attempt to regain it. These vested interests can relate to fear of financial loss – jobs, defined benefit schemes, stock options and, in the worst cases, to benefits gained from external sources not entirely sanctioned by the organisation. Perceived loss of internal or external status due to role redefinition or organisational restructuring is a common cause of resistance, as can be the threat of losing support for a pet project or activity.

In each case, identifying the resistance itself is the first challenge. Things are not always what they seem, and seemingly supportive individuals or teams can be covertly subversive. In these cases, one needs finely tuned antennae, links into the organisation and a good instinct to proactively identify the drag on momentum and progress towards integration goals. Your integration team must be similarly attuned to this risk. If projects just don't seem to be going anywhere, whether because they are inherently flawed or unnecessarily generate a steady flow of negativity, the red flag should be raised. Decoding the rationale behind any resistance can help to identify potential improvements to the project, or simply resistance for the sake of resistance (Ford & Ford, 2009). The skill of the integration leader is to know when concerns are potentially valid or represent an underlying symptom of fear and unwillingness to change.

And who knows – the resistance may indeed reflect a genuine flaw in your own thinking, or a disguised suggestion of how to improve your plans! The only way to find out is to take it on openly and constructively rather than ignore it and hope it will go away. Regardless of the cause, the more you listen, the easier you'll find it is to address.

The most influential individuals in groups, departments and cohorts are potentially the most important players in your 'coalition of change'. Equally, if not fully co-opted, they can and often will become dissidents, seeking to derail – or at least redirect – any integration activities they don't support. Authority comes in many forms, not only those formally defined and communicated within the organsiation. Be aware of who these key influencers are, seek them out and bring them over to your side early. Conversely, work to quickly immunise the integration process from disruptive influences, in extreme cases by removing them from the organisation entirely.

Act proactively and decisively to combat resistance, either by addressing underlying causes of anxiety head-on, or, if needs be, by removing intransigent sources of resistance.

Tackle the causes

What does it mean for me?

As the wheels of integration start to whirr into motion, it's easy to get caught up in the details of programme delivery. However, while the programme and what it will achieve are of huge importance to the business, these goals are almost certainly going to feel secondary to every individual working there relative to their personal concerns. No matter how committed people are to the new company and vision after Day One, no matter how senior they are, there is ultimately only one thing they *really* prioritise: themselves.

In a Harvard Business Review CEO Roundtable – "Lessons from Master Acquirers" – Dennis Kozlowski commented: "A very interesting statistic I once read says that people are normally productive for about 5.7 hours in an eight-hour business day. But any time a change of control takes place, their productivity falls to less than an hour. That holds true in merger situations. Inevitably, people immediately start thinking about themselves." (Carey, 2000).

'What about me' questions are the source of the most visceral anxieties. When shouting from the rooftops about the benefits of a transaction and the consequent integration, business leaders often instinctively take an organisational or shareholder standpoint. Left unanswered, and especially if perceived to be intentionally avoided, these 'what about me' questions can quickly turn from private apprehension into public resistance. Every individual making decisions on IT system changes, new policies, and of course organisational structures, has these questions hidden, usually quite deeply, underneath.

What about me?

While others certainly exist, individual concerns can usually be summed up by five questions: "Will I have a job?"; "Who will my new boss be?"; "Where will I work?"; "How will my pay and benefits change?" and "What are my longer term career prospects in the new organisation?"

People can't focus on 'what's right for the business' unless and until the personal questions have been settled, so answer them quickly and as openly as you can. Aon Hewitt found that a few months after an M&A process, the number of highly engaged employees tends to drop from a global baseline of 10% to a low of 5%, while the number of actively disengaged employees rises Aon Hewitt (2013).[2]

While quantifying such disengagement is difficult, it's not hard to argue that a lot of time and productivity is lost. This is not simply an issue of pure productivity: this malaise can impact safety (especially in industrial organisations); customer acquisition, sales and service; and of course retention of your key people. Competitors know that your business is at its weakest while going through an integration and the best of them will come after your customers, recruit your top talent and dent your reputation amongst stakeholders.

Counter this by creating a narrative to ease individual

2: *Managing Employee Engagement During Times of Change.* Aon Hewitt.

concerns. Even before you have the information needed to do this, you need to create some sort of certainty through your communications. Below we lay out the best way to alleviate anxieties throughout this initial tricky period, and to navigate the even harder times later when changes have to be made.

When personal concerns turn public

What could feasibly go wrong if you don't press your advantage and build momentum as soon as possible? What happens if you fail to recognise the importance of peoples' personal concerns? What happens if you misjudge the environment and context? At the very least, it's a real setback – but as shown below, the repercussions can be severe.

When working across different jurisdictions, it's important to understand the local culture and legal landscape. An oil and gas company's expansion in Africa through acquisition offers an object lesson. A central driving force behind their first deal was the acquisition of high quality technical capabilities and expertise, and the sharing of this capability with their existing local business. Despite this clear positive rationale, Day One was a non-event and post-close communications never took place. Consequently, the inherent value of the new people coming on board was never communicated to them, let alone the wider business. Before long rumours were spreading like wildfire that the acquirer's intention was, in fact, to fire every single employee in the newly-acquired company; an understandable assumption, as equivalent teams existed across all functions within the acquiring organisation.

Complicating the issue was the fact that, in this country, redundancy legislation protecting workers or guaranteeing severance pay on dismissal didn't exist; the new employees believed they were facing termination without a safety net. The acquirer underestimated the level of the anxiety and their lack of communication, regardless of their true intentions, only served to reinforce employee fears.

Fast forward a matter of days beyond Day One and the acquirer was handed a group lawsuit from its own new employees, seeking hundreds of thousands in redundancy payments in anticipation of termination. What seemed like a well-constructed acquisition and integration plan became a legal quagmire overnight, one which took months to unravel.

Understanding the potential underlying issues, in this case relating to local regulations, and communicating pre-emptively, was all that was needed to prevent the legal standoff. Furthermore, relationships with staff remained in intensive care for some time, delaying integration and delivery of the ultimate rationale behind the deal.

Communication needs to be about more than the business and plans for the future. In the days following acquisition, communications must focus on people. Only once personal concerns have been addressed will people be prepared to take the next step.

Who's staying?

Telling people who is staying or going is tricky to navigate, not least because you often can't be certain who you want to keep when you first walk into a company. One should at a minimum be aware pre-close of the roles that will exist within the new organisation and your plan for these roles as part of your operating model design. Sometimes, however, it is not possible to have the entire organisation designed down to the final role. Naturally, the objective is to design the organisation and its roles as quickly as possible after Day One – or faster.

Start from the top, and work down.

In the ideal scenario, you will have completed your detailed integration design before Day One, including your organisational structures. This is more likely to be possible in an 'agreed' (or 'friendly') transaction, where you'll have access to the organisation and can begin joint design work with the target or merger party. In this case, in the run-up to Day One, you'll have time to define the organisational model and structure, the core values, and the top team. Once you walk into the company, you can work quickly (within the constraints of local HR legislation) to communicate and implement your plans, filling in the blanks and making adjustments as the need arises.

Glaxo Wellcome and SmithKline Beecham

With the merger of these two pharmaceutical giants in 2001, the global regulatory review processes provided both organisations over six months to jointly conduct integration design and planning. Joint teams across all functional areas were assembled and worked together over the duration to understand each other's business and agree the right structure and way forward for the combined entity. While challenging from a communications and change management perspective, this situation paved the way for a relatively smooth merger, as the time between announcement and Day One was put to good use.

This is *the* ideal scenario – you can come out of the blocks and tell people if they have a job, their salary, to whom they report, where they'll work, and open up future career plan conversations. You remove uncertainty as quickly as possible, and immediately create the sense that you are in control and know what you're doing.

This ideal scenario however is rare. There are always unknowns and surprises that emerge after Day One – and you should never assume otherwise! Departments and divisions will want an opportunity to define, or at least influence, their own structure once the top team is set, people leave unexpectedly, and so on.

Populating the necessary roles means assessing not only who

has the requisite skillset, but also how committed they are to the journey, and how well they'll fit in with the team. This presents an important, once-in-a-deal opportunity to kill two birds with one stone: get them involved in developing the operating model itself. Not only do you get their input, but it provides a unique insight into their enthusiasm and motivation and gives them a sense of involvement in their future – a key component of any effort to gain support for change. A formal organisational alignment, design and planning exercise should be initiated as soon as possible, even prior to transaction close if circumstances allow. Ideally, and especially in a merger, this review should be conducted across both organisations if there is to be a high degree of integration across all functions.

Organisational or operating model design exercises come in as many forms as there are consulting firms, so its important to select a group, process and methodology that suits you and your organisation's culture and focuses on those areas relevant to deal benefits and long-term strategy. While their main objective is to provide structure and external insight into your design and planning for the new organisational model, these processes have many benefits if designed carefully. They act as a strong mechanism for spreading the values and culture of the acquiring organisation, can provide deep insight into both organisational and business issues, create opportunities to observe individuals in problem-solving mode and, importantly, send a clear signal that you are willing to listen. For this reason, don't short-change the exercise – it is after all defining your future business and how it will deliver your deal objectives, so invest the time, leadership and resources to ensure these and other benefits are achieved.

Consultants can be helpful in guiding you through this process, one which should include multiple interviews across and deep into the organisation, supplemented by group working sessions and feedback opportunities. To be effective, such exercises require heavy involvement from the acquirer's team – or the relevant future leader of the department or operating unit – including some senior management. This will require agreed interview templates, perhaps some training and/or support from integration or organisational design professionals. But, as the responsibility for designing and making a success of the new merged entity lies with your *line* managers, they will do well to be deeply involved in this crucial process.

Unsolicited ('hostile') transactions are by their very nature much more difficult, as you generally don't have access to the organisation prior to transaction close and there is no ability for the two organisations' management teams to collaborate. While there are ways to learn something about the target, e.g. by taking on former employees as advisors or consultants, as discussed in Chapter 2, it is unlikely that you'll have all the answers by Day One.

That awkward phase: What to say in the meantime

As described above, transactions in which detailed access is not possible before transaction close – sometimes also the case for so called 'friendly' transactions – will require a period *after* transaction close in which to undertake the work required to design the new organisation. This is a high-risk period. You own the business and have to run it effectively while uncertainty is rampant and, at the same time, conduct an inclusive, robust organisational design exercise. It is crucial to be pragmatic and minimise the variables by announcing the top team immediately, communicating clearly when the detailed answers will come, isolating the operating teams from the change process and moving fast, fast, fast.

In the meantime, keep your story clear and stick to it.

Settle nerves

You can gain trust in small but significant ways. Tell people you will honour their contracts, as presumably you are legally bound to do. Despite the legal obligation, it is not uncommon for staff to believe the acquirer will find ways to circumvent their contracts. In this case, stating what seems obvious to you goes a long way to providing some relief.

The next thing to do is create certainty around the process. You can't provide all the answers your nervous and rumour-buffeted staff require. Provide them at least with clarity on the process – tell them *when* you'll tell them. This is where the content and style of your communication programme comes to the fore. In other words, if you can't tell people the answer, try to let them know what you're doing to get it. Sketch out – and keep to – timetable of when you will know the answers, how often they can expect feedback, and where to go if they have any questions or concerns. Hold 'town hall' meetings well beyond Day One to present and discuss progress and challenges.

Communications needs to be targeted at both a company-wide and an individual level.

An important tool for ensuring no one falls between the cracks, either in being communicated with, or in confirming their place in (or outside) the organisation, is to assign each acquired individual impacted by integration to one of your integration team. *Each and every* staff member should have an integration team leader alongside their name. The team leader's role in this instance is to hold the necessary conversations with their assigned staff member, understand their role, capabilities and preferences and contribute this insight to the organisational review process.

Prioritise top talent

During this period, people may seek an exit themselves before you've come to your own decision about them. If any such person has already been identified as key for the future of the business, they should become a priority. In the first instance, telling them they are an important part of the future is vital. Understanding the source of their discontent is the first step in creating a plan to keep them.

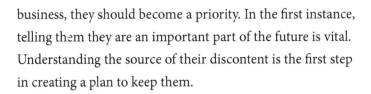

It's <u>not</u> all about the money.

Retention bonuses can act as a disincentive when combined with a lack of communication. When one senior technical individual with huge potential and institutional knowledge was offered a retention bonus, the reasoning was poorly communicated. The use of a mid-term incentive made him believe they were only thinking of his usefulness for the mid-term; at no point had they discussed their plans for the long-term and his role 'on the bus'. Consequently, feeling increasingly negative towards his new managers and his long-term prospects in the new business, he started looking for jobs elsewhere.

Integration team leaders are fundamental in determining who is a 'keeper' and ensuring the relevant conversations are held with these individuals to minimise the risk of a precipitous flight into the arms of your competitors.

Occasionally, retention bonuses will need to be offered. Your dialogue should recognise their desire to leave but point out that they haven't given you sufficient time to demonstrate that you can create a role and career opportunity for them. Beyond this, a retention bonus linked to specific objectives can be

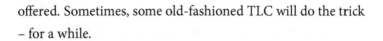

offered. Sometimes, some old-fashioned TLC will do the trick – for a while.

A common but bad practice is to offer blanket retention bonuses not linked to specific objectives. Simply offering a cash incentive to stay for six months encourages people to do just that: stay for six months, putting in minimal effort, and spending their days looking for their next job to start in month seven. You can't blame them – you've incentivised them to do just that. Linking their package to the delivery of certain objectives encourages them to work optimally and focus their efforts on supporting integration or business performance. At worst, they can help you through a tricky period, after which they will take their package and leave. At best, they could be convinced to stay after the initial retention period.

Bonuses like this should be used sparingly, and in fact are far more widespread than they need to be. They're only for key individuals motivated by cash, and only when you've identified that you really need them. If someone really wants to leave, not only is it difficult to stop them, but after a certain point it is unwise, as they could negatively influence the environment and other employees.

And remember that it's not all about the money. Individuals are motivated by many different things other than cash, which is typically 'top five' but rarely 'number one'. The role, career opportunities, status, work environment, location – all these and more are the real drivers of engagement. Understand, person by person, what will make each individual stay and perform, and tailor your *individual* retention strategy accordingly.

Don't lie, don't hide

Throughout the communications process, one rule is unbreakable: never lie to individuals about their future.

The most 'innocent' of lies can be damaging. When someone approaches a member of the executive team and asks whether they think they're likely to have a job in a month's time, the natural human tendency is to try and comfort them and alleviate an awkward situation. Saying 'if it was up to me I'd keep you but bear in mind that I don't make the final decision' may not even be a lie, but it's unhelpful.

Whatever happens, don't give people false hope. Not only is it dishonest, but it can give a serial acquirer a poor reputation, making it even harder to build trust. Make sure your entire team is provided with clear, unambiguous direction, or even a script – usually focusing on the process – to deal with the inevitable questions about individuals' futures. This will make it easier for them to avoid the tendency to placate and will send a consistent message across the organisation.

Bad news is better than no news

Contrary to the idiom, no news is bad news in integration and change processes. Stick to the deadlines by which you promised updates, and communicate regularly and frequently throughout the process. Once you have your operating model and organisational structure, you need your communications to address both groups and individuals depending on their level of seniority. At this point you can start to tell people who has a job, and also fill in the blanks regarding the work environment – the future of a division, who'll run it, where it will be, and so on. Don't fall into the trap of, "We have nothing significant to communicate this month, so let's not". In fact, a steady ship on course is an excellent and important message to give – be brief, but let people know that 'everything's going according to plan'.

In a bizarre sort of a way, bad news – such as the departure of one or more individuals, or even missed deadlines or unexpected issues – is settling, as long as it is positioned within a logical framework and aligns with the overall narrative. Perhaps counter-intuitively, while 'no news is bad news', 'bad news is helpful' as it demonstrates that you're being open and honest, and so builds trust and credibility – provided of course you have a plan to address whatever problems you've raised. If something has gone wrong, the grapevine will ensure that people know about it anyway, so controlling the story is always better than ignoring it. Releasing such information is the only way to counteract the rumour mill by providing data points with which to fill the voids with your own perspective, decisions and plans. There is nothing more unsettling than a surprise, uncommunicated departure – the inexplicably empty desk that confronts staff in the morning. This brings you to the next stage of the process.

Pull the trigger

You've navigated through Day One. You've formulated a plan. What's left? The hardest part. Once you've decided who's staying and who's going, you need to tell them as soon as possible, even if that means telling people months before you actually want them out the door.

Some oppose this line of thinking. Perhaps you need continuity for a few months after Day One, and it's too soon to start unsettling people? Maybe you'll squeeze an extra drop of productivity out of them if they think they're proving themselves? But, while this may offer short-term gains, the long-term loss typically vastly outweighs this.

Like a bandage, it's best to minimise the organisation's pain by removing it as quickly as possible. Even during a handover period, better to tell people that their role going into the future will become redundant, but ask them to stay throughout the transition and give them the right incentives where necessary. Often, deferring their notice period to the end and guaranteeing their exit package, irrespective of the length of the transitionary period, is sufficient to secure their support.

Treating people this way will have positive effects on the entire organisation, especially those who have been selected to stay. Rolling or drip-fed layoffs – common in financial services organisations – simply create a permanent state of anxiety and disaffection, neither of which are conducive to high-performing organisations. Get the job done once and for all (or within the reasonable confines of organisational evolution).

Out with the old...

Even though you should tell people about the future of their role as soon as possible, a handover period is often needed for roles where people need time to bed in, helping to ensure the fundamental business doesn't fall over while the organisation transitions to a new model. What's more, each department will have its own schedule for handover, varying from business to business.

The other factor when considering the length of any transition is the sensitivity of the functions being performed, the information to which people have access and the potential for destructive action. For example, in financial services acquisitions, keeping surplus IT staff for a lengthy transition period is often frowned upon as an unnecessary cost. Such considerations and traditional practices are central to the design of any handover. Similarly, anyone holding strong relationships with customers, e.g. sales executives, may need to be retained for a longer period of time, but only if you are certain they are not likely to poison the well with their future employment in mind.

One final piece of advice before we conclude this chapter. If any former owners or executives aren't staying with the new business for the long-term, get them out the door on Day One. There's a common view that you should retain the old CEO or Finance Director as a special advisor or consultant during any such handover period. After all, they know how the business runs, they hold many of the key customer relationships, and they're well-respected by the team. They've said they'll be happy to 'stay on a bit' to help with the transition, or worse still, they are staying on as part of an earn-out arrangement that ties them, and their performance, to the business for several years post-close.

The problem here is twofold. First, keeping them on, even if their title and role has changed on paper, presents employees with a picture of confused accountability. No one is quite sure to whom they should go when they have questions or problems. It's (understandably, inevitably) hard for former CEOs to resist the temptation to get involved in these kinds of affairs. It's equivalent to having a former football manager hang around in the dressing room after they've been sacked. You need to be decisive in distancing old executives from the business.

Second, if this individual has been retained with specific operational responsibility, ensuring they fit into – and genuinely support – your plans and culture for the new, combined business is essential. A former business owner or CEO/CFO who enthusiastically supports the new strategy and leads his or her team in your stated direction as opposed to their historical one is a rare individual. What is more common is for such individuals with a vested interest in the past to actively or subconsciously resist changes to 'their' business, underperform, and eventually wish to leave. Even if their intent is to adopt the new strategy and direction wholeheartedly, it is worth understanding whether the skills and capabilities they brought to the organisation in the past are actually relevant to where you intend to take it in the future.

Rather than 'hoping for the best', it is generally better to launch and complete the handover fully and quickly. For many of the same reasons – and contrary to common practice – earnouts should be avoided unless you are truly certain the individuals have a long-term future with the new business. That doesn't mean former MDs or CEOs can have no role post-close, but it must be carefully crafted to 'release' the acquisition from the old and 'unfreeze' the team's resistance to change, while still retaining access to key relationships and institutional knowledge. 'On call' consultancy agreements work well, but without the corner office.

KEY CONCEPTS:

1. **Momentum is the lifeblood of a successful integration programme – keep an eye on the momentum and take action if the programme appears to be stalling.**

    a. **Move quickly, more quickly than feels comfortable;**

    b. **Pursue early victories – pick the low-hanging fruit to signal change and momentum;**

    c. **Actively monitor, evaluate and manage resistance;**

    d. **Address the 'me' issues as quickly as you can.**

2. **Always communicate with integrity – even if it means sharing bad news.**

3. **Secure your key talent early – they can also become valuable advocates of the process.**

4. **Complete any restructuring as soon as you have the data you need – delaying simply creates further uncertainty, anxiety and resistance.**

5. **Pay special attention to former owners or senior executives you wish to retain – and do so only under specific, well-crafted conditions.**

Chapter 5:
OPPORTUNITY AND RISK: THE GEMINI TWINS OF INTEGRATION

"Planning is an unnatural process; it is much more fun to do something. And the nicest thing about not planning is that failure comes as a complete surprise rather than being preceded by a period of worry and depression."

JOHN HARVEY JONES, BUSINESSMAN (1924–2008)

"One thing at least Paul knew he'd got absolutely right. Integration planning was conducted early pre-close, exhaustive, and taken to a level of detail surpassing even his own initial expectations; execution of the programme post-close had been almost flawless. This was especially important given Quintado's board – and even some of his executive colleagues – had seemed almost carelessly relaxed about what exactly needed to happen post-close and lost interest almost the day after closing. After all, they kept saying, "this deal is a strategic no-brainer", with obvious synergies and benefits that would start flowing the minute both companies were "batting on the same side". How hard could it be?

Even then Paul knew the answer: "Much harder than you think". Thankfully he found in Samina, the appointed Integration Director, the perfect person to lead integration post-close: Experienced and detail-oriented, her success against all odds in last year's SAP rollout gave her credibility across Quintado, despite the occasional complaint from his people at the time that the programme itself had become a 'paper factory'. OK, so some of the project management rigour she enforced across the entire company wasn't fully understood by everyone (even Paul didn't quite get the point of a weekly Earned Value Analysis review or the Change Control Board she established), but it worked well for the SAP implementation, and it worked well here – milestones were being met and the project was coming in well under budget.

...and yet, while the operation appeared to be succeeding, the patient was getting worse. Time to talk to Samina about what additional controls and resources she might need."

An acquisition or merger is almost by definition an exercise in dreaming big. When justifying such high-risk endeavours, hyperbole about the opportunities abound. Deal benefits take centre stage, and while the risks are generally raised, they are often ignored, or at least glossed over. Transactions are generally optimistic affairs – especially for the acquirer. After all, effective teams are motivated by positive outcomes, milestones met and targets achieved.

Perversely, once integration planning is underway, some acquirers go to extreme lengths to 'guarantee' post-close success by planning every detail and contingency, charting the course of integration to the millimetre. Such groups typically go on to define success as adherence to the plan, on-time achievement of milestones and 'zero tolerance' to deviation of any kind. New processes and systems are comprehensively designed and implemented, and mechanisms established to manage risks and issues so tightly that nothing will go wrong from Day One to integration completion. Often different from the deal team, groups responsible for delivering the integration see themselves as compensating for the over-optimism of those who pulled the deal together.

"Great, where's the problem?", you might ask. The challenge is that, in many organisations, a healthy balance between these two views is never achieved, deal after deal. As both 'sides' in the opportunity/risk debate seek to justify their positions (both regarding the deal and their own roles), the force between them only increases. Like any tug-of-war, this tension never ends with everyone grouped around a healthy middle ground. Instead the outcome takes everyone to one side – "This deal will be smooth and easy, no need to worry!", or to the other – "This deal is going to be the death of us unless we get it absolutely perfectly right". Neither extreme will result in an optimal outcome for your integration.

First, let's consider what's at stake.

Integration is about opportunity and risk in equal measure. So, just as you need to seek, define and analyse those activities that will deliver deal value, so must you also identify the risks that can derail the integration and put in place explicit and detailed plans to mitigate these risks should they arise.

Sometimes executive and integration teams pursuing a transaction or preparing for integration simply shrug off the risks – success bias leads people to think that with their personal experience and skillset the integration cannot flounder or fail. Perhaps they don't wish the risks to dilute the benefits of the transaction or erode deal momentum. Others simply don't like to consider the possibility of the unexpected or the risky. So what risks should you be paying attention to?

The first thing we should point out is that by integration risk, we are not referring only to outright integration failure. Academia and the media are replete with examples of failed M&A, especially where the integration itself led to a destruction in company value. Concern over this is justifiable – overall global M&A success rates continue to be disappointing at best. However, if the original transaction and integration due diligence has been carried out correctly, the root causes of outright failure – such as culture clash or lack of understanding of what you're buying – are much less likely to come as a surprise.

Typically, when we think of risks we tend to conjure images

of some catastrophic operational failure, the loss of a
major customer, or worse, a fatal or debilitating safety or
environmental incident during the integration process.

In practice however, general *underperformance* relative to
the targets articulated in the integration plan or transaction
business case is the bigger challenge. Achieving the benefits
you originally set out and meeting their corresponding
targets is largely contingent on the effective planning and
management of integration itself. Shareholders have become
increasingly sensitised to integration risk and demand
well-planned integrations from their executive teams
undertaking deals. Equally, they are unforgiving if the targets
communicated at the start are not met in time, or at all. Public
listed companies are particularly exposed to the ire of the
markets and other shareholders should they be perceived
to be bungling a post-transaction integration. On the other
hand, companies that repeatedly demonstrate their prowess
at acquiring and smoothly integrating targets are given a freer
rein to pursue subsequent deals.

The inherent uncertainties and challenges accompanying
any deal are the reason competent serial acquirers ensure
their integration capability is institutionalised and, in large
part, reflects their experience of risks and how to avoid or
mitigate them. The overt benefit of institutionalising a risk-
aware culture is that it helps business leaders identify, contain
and manage key risks before they crystallise and become

debilitating. Beyond this, though, there is the psychological benefit of you and your team knowing you have the right mechanisms in place to foresee and, most importantly, *adapt*, to risks that arise. Consequently, momentum is maintained.

So, how do you go about achieving this?

M&A Risk – A three-sided coin

It goes without saying that insufficient consideration of risk for whatever reason is vital to avoid. Less obvious are the types of risk that you need to consider.

The first port of call is, of course, integration plan risks – risks associated with the execution of the integration programme itself. Frequently this is the only type of risk acquirers consider; to their cost, as we'll discuss later.

Risks related to successfully delivering the integration programme itself include items as varied as:

- Risk of the integration programme stalling and losing momentum;
- Failure to receive the necessary agreements with local and national governments;
- Inability to deliver the cost reductions or synergies in time or to the level anticipated when the transaction was approved;
- Delays to individual integration tasks, leading to a cascade of slipping milestones, missed deadlines, and increased cost.

Regardless of root cause, the most incapacitating, in our experience, is the risk of loss of momentum. The early stages of the integration programme – the first 30-day programme, the first 100 days, the first sixth months – must be shaped and prioritised around quick wins and early enablers of future benefit (such as changes to organisational structures and alignment of product strategies).

Less well considered however is a second category of risk: the distraction and stress your integration will place on your ability to conduct day-to-day business. Examples include:

- IT system vulnerabilities introduced as a result of integration of the two companies' networks and applications;

- Loss of control over cash, credit card charges, bank accounts;

- Existing functions spread too thin due to their staff's involvement in the integration process;

- Impact on material contracts – including employment contracts – resulting from a change in ownership.

Business as usual is crucial in this context. Any executive team will (or certainly should) have risk registers in which they are formally tracking the biggest risks their business faces. Surprisingly few, however, consider how these risks change – usually for the worse – through a period of significant business transformation. Day-to-day activities essential to a company's survival should be factored into this category of risk assessment. If you eliminate corporate roles that appear redundant, will aspects of a core process fall through the cracks? Will you forget to pay a supplier? Will your new billing system prevent you from collecting money from your newly-acquired customers? Does your insurance properly cover the expanded business? Will you remember to renew your licenses? When everything in your company is in flux, there is ample opportunity for you to overlook some fundamental elements of your operations that keep it running and provide competitive advantage – workload, focus, capital expenditure and more.

The final area of risk often not considered is how the external environment may impact your delivery of deal benefits. One easily-avoided risk in international deals is poor contingency planning for exchange rate volatility – we've witnessed this destroy more than one acquisition business case post-close without anything changing on the ground whatsoever. Taking another example, consider the reaction of your competitors to your organisation undergoing a major integration programme. For them, a major merger or acquisition could (and should) pose an enormous threat – but at the same time, the integration process itself may offer opportunities to these same competitors. They may target key employees who they suspect will become uncertain or unhappy about their future, or opportunistically pursue key customers or markets while your focus is elsewhere.

Other common issues arise when key stakeholders such as

suppliers, trade unions, governments and NGOs, see the transaction and integration process as an opportunity to reset their relationship with the newly-created combined entity. Suppliers may may try to re-establish an advantage in pricing or payment terms, while trade unions may take the opportunity to roll back agreements or change the tone of the dialogue with management, especially towards the end of existing agreements. Furthermore, unanticipated hostile reaction to your transaction by stakeholders such as local communities or regulators, can place enormous stress on the management team and employees. Mitigation plans and scenarios must be carefully defined and 'war gamed' to change the balance between success and failure.

Other risks will, of course, be specific to your industry, strategy, integration plan and context. In an industrial company, they could relate to safety or environmental practices, while in a consumer business they may relate to unanticipated negative impacts on brand and consumer engagement – or even to day-to-day delivery of products to the retail outlets.

More dangerous are the risks that can impair your strategic positioning, such as the loss of key market, a major industrial accident, or damaging relations with local or national governmental groups.

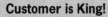

Customer is King!

A major drinks manufacturer acquired a maintenance company that installed and maintained drink vending machines in fast-food restaurants. Once they had completed the deal, they decided to include the new business in the scope of an ongoing project aimed at moving their warehouse management to a third-party logistics provider. The acquired company's operations had historically relied upon a simple but effective stock management system.

This was then replaced when the outsourcing project hit in the midst of the storm of other integration activity. Predictably, the target's previous excellent customer service record deteriorated rapidly as response times lengthened.

Over-complicating the integration caused unnecessary damage to the company's ability to satisfy its customers, and consequently endangered profitability and their hard-won reputation.

Confronting and mitigating risk: Make a plan, and make it live

Most larger companies retain risk registers to identify key risks in their operations and put plans in place to actively manage them. Risks are rated by likelihood, with avoidance and/or mitigation plans attached to each. A second assessment is then conducted to estimate the change in likelihood or impact with their respective management plan in place. A second assessment is then conducted to estimate the change in likelihood or impact with their respective management plan in place.

Creating a Risk Register: Example

The international standard on risk management uses a 5x5 matrix:

Likelihood Rating					
5	11	16	20	23	25
4	7	12	17	21	24
3	4	8	13	18	22
2	2	5	9	14	19
1	1	3	6	10	15
	1	2	3	4	5
	Consequence Rating				

Standard practice is to assign ratings to both likelihood and consequence by predefining the criteria for each level. For example, for a scenario to rank as level-5 consequence in a natural resource company, the following may need to apply:

5	Rating
$100m+ loss or gain	**Financial impact US$ EBIT**
$20m+	**Property Damage US$**
$600m + loss or gain	**Investment Return US$ NPV**
• Multiple fatalities and/or • Significant irreversible effects to 10's of people.	**Health and Safety**
• Category 5 – an incident that has caused disastrous environmental impact with long term effect requiring major remediation.	**Environment**
• Prominent negative International media coverage over several days. • Significant negative impact on share price for months.	**Community / Reputation**
• Major litigation or prosecution with damages of $50m+ plus significant costs. • Custodial sentence for company Executive • Prolonged closure of operations by authorities.	**Legal and Compliance**

Once these relevant consequence and likelihood ratings are defined, mitigation plans must be developed in an effort to reduce both factors.

An integration process is no different – it needs its own risk register, one that seeks to anticipate how an integration process (or the business) could go awry post-close and how it may impact day-to-day operations or delivery of deal value. Creating and maintaining the risk register is typically the role of the integration director, while the Integration Steering Committee must vet and monitor this register throughout the integration process.

By definition a post-acquisition or merger integration process is a major disruption of the status quo, and this necessitates revisiting the risk register on a regular basis, continuously keeping it targeted on both your integration and your ongoing business. Risks identified as part of your integration planning may no longer be relevant and new risks can arise. The process of refreshing risks registers is itself a useful discipline to remind the integration team of the need to remain vigilant and keep their avoidance and mitigation plans updated. Furthermore, they serve to drive continuous re-prioritisation of your risks, helping to separate the wood from the trees and preventing the team from the time-consuming distraction of managing every risk simply because it appears to be current and important to someone especially vocal in the business.

Countless books have been written on how to manage risk, and the principles and processes for this are no different for integration. Brainstorming and analysing risks, generating and maintaining risks logs, and using both to actively manage your risks alongside programme delivery are good, solid first steps. But in many cases, this effort never leaves the platform simply because of a lack of direct accountability, not for management of the risk process, but for the individual risks themselves.

For every major risk, make sure there is a single owner with responsibility to develop mitigation or avoidance plans, conduct the avoidance activities, keep tabs on any early warning indicators and – should the risk be triggered – activate and manage the mitigation plan. Ensure that the current status of all key risks – and their owners – is clearly and explicitly referenced in any Steering Committee reports or equivalent documents and meetings; nothing keeps people more on point than knowing that their boss' boss is looking.

Finally, ensure that every integration team leader and member is aware that, even if they have successfully pulled off numerous integrations before, every situation is unique and even the simplest risks should be discussed and planned for. Xstrata's acquisition of a large Australian mining company offers a perfect example of the impact of complacency. One of the business units had successfully integrated numerous acquisitions in the past and depended on their collective experience and intuition, rather than what they considered to be the bureaucratic burden of detailed risk registers and risk management plans. Weeks into the acquisition, the roof of one of the acquired mines collapsed, taking an expensive piece of equipment out of commission and impacting production for months. Fortunately there were no injuries, but the lesson proved clear and costly.

A rule of thumb

Depending of course on the acquisition business case and integration priorities, as well as the structure and nature of the company, we've found it best to try and distance your front-office teams – those involved in mission-critical areas such as production and sales – from the disruption of integration.

For example, if you've acquired a company with two business units and a head office, it is likely that there will be a large overlap between the activities of the two head offices, whereas the business units may operate in distinct markets or deliver different products or services. It makes sense, therefore, that your immediate priority should be to focus on eradicating the redundant activities across the two sets of corporate functions, while permitting the business units to continue to operate with as little interference as possible. Key to this approach, though, is the understanding of how activities in the corporate function relate to each business unit – the 'umbilical cords' of (typically) strategic planning, budgeting, finance, treasury, IT and HR. Once these areas are mapped out in detail, a plan can be devised to remove these links from the acquired head office and connect them into the newly unified corporate office.

This approach of insulating the operating units from the detailed work of unifying the corporate functions aims to ensure that the units generating the revenue and profits remain operational throughout, isolated from the risks of disruption.

Naturally, if the acquisition or merger is predicated on combining two or more businesses units in the same market or product spaces to bring about scale benefits or a broader market reach, once cannot ignore the need to integrate these units. Nevertheless, the benefits of minimising the distraction of corporate processes coming together remains valid, even while integration activities are pursued within the operating businesses. In any case, reducing the changes hitting your front-line staff from every direction is central to helping them stay focused on keeping the lights on and delivering the business.

For example, let's consider the common initiatives required when two major retail banks integrate. Sequencing of the various streams of integration should be given detailed attention. One might wish to focus on rolling out a common brand identity across the newly combined banking network, while integrating back-office activities such as IT systems and treasury processes, but delay the detailed rollout of a new, uniform set of branch activities to ensure customers continue to enjoy good service from their familiar branches.

Keep it simple, but make them own it

Recognising and dealing with integration risk is actually deceptively simple. In effect, it resides in ensuring that everyone involved, from the bottom up, recognises the change in your risk profile that comes as a result of the integration and the different ways these new risks might impact their ability to get their own job done.

Once you've achieved this, integration risks become much like normal business risks, with major ones being assigned to the individuals best placed to manage them.

Most risks are typically the result of simple omissions or complacency, and are therefore avoidable with a little forethought and planning. The process of ongoing risk mapping and tracking can go a long way to identifying the areas of potential vulnerability and keeping individuals and teams sensitised to the potential for things to go wrong.

Adapt to an ever-changing environment

So far, we've drawn out the importance of being proactive in risk management. However, good risk management goes beyond the numerous frameworks for identifying and managing risks; it demands a fundamental change in mindset.

Particularly in an integration, you need to be both vigilant and versatile – risk is not something that can be analysed and then shelved, only to be revisited if or when an identified risk manifests. Instead, it demands constant vigilance and versatility to deal with its many and varied forms, faces and impacts as they arise.

Integration is a programme, not a project

Even more than typical transformation or restructuring programmes, integrations begin their journey rife with unknowns and uncertainties. The first few months often reveal, and force a rethink on, personal agendas across the new team, hidden process and system complexities, unexpected customer reactions, culture and role 'discontinuities' at odds with documented structures and accountabilities, and more. And that's not considering the mis-steps and outright mistakes the integration and operating teams will invariably make along the way.

Successful integration programmes demand *perception* to spot the unexpected; *anticipation* of things that won't play out as intended; and *agility* to adjust your approach and plans as circumstances – or your understanding of them – change.

This situation requires that you understand and apply the principles of good *programme* management alongside good *project* management. Build an environment in which ambiguity and change is expected, so that the programme can adapt to it, rather than try to control, ignore or eliminate it. Focus on delivery of benefits, not simply the achievement of milestones: important as they may be, they are only intermediate steps to a higher goal. If a different, better route to reaching your deal benefits emerges (and it often does), you need to be ready and able to take it. Ensure someone on the team – ideally the Integration Director – is spending formal time 'looking out' to ensure they understand how the environment or ecosystem in which integration is taking place is altering, where new opportunities are appearing to deliver value, and how to shift your programme priorities and structure to accommodate them all.

Prioritise for value and risk

How does an already stretched integration team manage all these demands, potential risks and enticing value opportunities, while trying to keep the ship on an even keel and responsive to the changing winds of fortune post-close?

Relentless prioritisation, of course.

An integration programme will fail if the process and deliverables are divorced from or tenuously connected to the key sources of value creation – synergies, cost reductions, efficiency improvements, new capabilities and markets, and so on – and, equally, the core risks.

You need to identify where the company will benefit from the deal and define your integration specifically to deliver these benefits. This can also involve recognising where there is no need to integrate, or where benefits can be achieved in a simpler, less risky way. Integrating for the sake of it is all too common, and regularly damages the business. At the very least, you will distract an already stretched integration team from its true priorities.

Clarifying objectives

Following the merger of two large steel companies, a team was brought in to design the operating model for the integration of the central corporate functions. This activity was conducted entirely separate to – in fact wholly disconnected from – the integration and benefits realisation initiatives taking place across the rest of the organisation. With no clear objectives or desired benefits anchoring the corporate integration, the exercise drifted – how could anyone agree what the corporate centre should look like if no one understood what it was supposed to achieve?

This serves as a textbook example of what not to do when planning any integration. Integration needs to be firmly driven by deal benefits to ensure clarity, alignment and buy-in by those tasked to deliver it.

Despite what may appear as self-evident conventional wisdom, a small finance department will not necessarily need to upgrade their systems to align with your global ERP standard if doing so delivers no deal benefit, adds complexity and damages their productivity, especially if the department is able to function with its existing systems. Leave this task to another day.

It's very difficult to anticipate and capitalise on the unexpected when perfection is the watchword of every aspect of your integration. The best integration programmes, ones that are focused on accelerating deal benefits, understand that 'good enough delivered now' is almost always better than 'ideal delivered in 12 months'. Don't strive for perfection. While inclusion of the new entity's finance function into the acquirer's global SAP embrace may be ideal and ultimately preferred, it's also costly, distracting and seldom, in our experience, central to the delivery of an acquisition business case. Instead, build solutions – new processes, ways of working, even IT systems – that help the businesses work together sooner rather than later; even in the full knowledge that the interim solution may have to be discarded at some point in the future.

When the going gets tough, the momentum and motivation to push through should come from the top. Conversely, the root cause of underperformance tends to be a lack of senior attention or resource applied to the programme. People will look to their boss to judge how they should be prioritising their workload, and if senior management aren't sufficiently committed to the integration then you can't really expect anyone else to care. Similarly, if senior management can't apply the right resources, don't prioritise appropriately, and become severely overworked, concluding integration successfully become immeasurably harder.

Either way, the end result is the same – individual projects stall and are eventually forgotten, and integration begins to drift into the long grass. Take any department you can think of: you might be combining policies and procedures, bringing organisational structures together, or just moving towards one IT platform. If these things only partly happen, you end up with a superficial, incomplete result. The new department is integrated in name only, but now also graced with an extra layer of half-implemented ways of working and confused accountabilities. The can has been kicked down the road, only to reappear sometime in the future.

Ultimately, this all comes down to two very simple – but difficult – tasks for the business and integration leadership: ensuring clear accountability, and encouraging strong teamwork. In this chapter, we've highlighted the need for accountability in risk management; in the next, we'll discuss how to build and maintain strong teams.

KEY CONCEPTS:

1. Pay attention to the potential risks:

   a. Risks related to potential failure of the integration process itself;

   b. Normal business risks exacerbated by the integration programme; and

   c. Risks emanating from external impacts and responses to your transaction.

2. Build integration-specific risk registers; make them living documents to help ingrain a risk-aware culture within all programme participants.

3. Insulate the people and processes on the front line – sales and production in particular – from remote integration activities where possible. Sequence integration to minimise disruption to the customer experience.

4. Re-prioritise continuously and relentlessly:

   a. Make your objectives clear to all and use these to define integration activities and priorities;

   b. Focus on deal value and risk – let both guide the allocation of your resources throughout the process;

   c. Do not attempt to build the perfect company in every respect from Day One;

   d. Do what's necessary to bring the combined entity to a

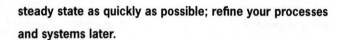

steady state as quickly as possible; refine your processes
and systems later.

5. Expect the unexpected and allow time for it. Build flexibility
into your plans so that you can sustain programme
momentum despite the inevitable unexpected events.

Chapter 6:
BUILD POWERFUL TEAMS AND MAKE THEM ACCOUNTABLE

"Teamwork is the ability to work together toward a common vision; the ability to direct individual accomplishments toward organisational objectives. It is the fuel that allows common people to attain uncommon results."

ANDREW CARNEGIE

"The Programme Dashboard was showing 'green' across the board, and almost every milestone was being hit on schedule… and yet somehow everyone knew (or at least felt) that the integration wasn't working. The environment of 'us and them' was worsening, and every time Paul called a meeting to understand and tackle the hot spots, getting people to raise their hands to solve the increasing snowball of problems was a challenge. Having now spoken to Samina, it was clear that the formal programme was tracking only part of what was really going on, only part of what was important to deliver the acquisition business case. Paul's frustration was rising, but a way forward was beginning to emerge in his mind: he needed to get his senior team to step up to the up to the plate,

work together to provide a single, company-wide view of how integration was going, and take collective responsibility for delivering every element of the business case. Even calling them a 'senior team' was wrong: at this stage some of them were barely on speaking terms and most of his time seemed to be spent defusing one argument after another. This wasn't going to be easy."

It goes without saying that creating effective teams is one of the most important actions you will undertake when bringing together individuals from two distinct organisations to create a new operating unit or new company. After all, your organisation delivers through teams of all types on a day-to-day basis – no effective teams, no business (see Chapter 1 for advice on picking your team).

What is less obvious, however, is how hard it is to do in the heat of a post-acquisition or merger integration setting. We are expecting – demanding, even – that individuals who before Day One were in separate organisations, suddenly come together in harmony and deliver the purpose and profitability of the newly-combined entity. Regardless of their experience, their role in the new business, or even their experience living through prior acquisitions, these are uncharted waters for the people who will make up these new teams. Bringing together two different companies to create one means that individuals leading the new teams will be confronted with new ideas, processes and environments, in a newly-formed group made up of individuals whom they may have never met. They may even be people who see themselves as professional 'enemies', sharing a level of mistrust and being highly protective of their own ways of working.

Getting these individuals to overcome their biases and prejudices – of each other, the integration itself and sometimes even the stated direction of the new organisation – is a priority.

One part of the solution can include team-building activities and events. These may include off-sites involving some kind of extreme sporting activity, interspersed with long, alcohol-laced dinners. It can also include the use of psychometric or personality profiling tools to help individuals gain an insight into each other's natural styles and approaches. These can involve facilitated sessions in which a team-building expert observes the dynamics of the new team and provides feedback and tools for improving interactions. The plethora of approaches that have emerged over the past decade or two offers the executive an overwhelming set of choices to improve interpersonal dynamics and build new teams.

While undoubtedly helpful, 'pure' team building is not a panacea. While many of these techniques have a role in team development during integration, our experience is that, when undertaken outside the context of the business and devoid of the content of real issues and decision-making, their benefit can be superficial and short-lived. Effective, functional teams come together most effectively and quickly by tackling live business issues, observing each other's decision-making styles in real-time and gaining insight into the mental models shaping their new colleagues' biases. An experienced facilitator can be extremely helpful in kick-starting and accelerating what is often an awkward start to a new team's journey; and in keeping team members focused on key business decisions.

Focusing solely on team building, however, will have limited success when the team's issues go beyond lack of time and experience with each other. If the belief creeps in that fundamental differences between the teams are impeding their ability to gel, you need to respond.

At is most basic, team building is about two things: helping groups of people work together towards a common goal; and creating the right conditions and structures to enable them to be what every good team is – greater than the sum of its parts. This chapter considers both aspects as they apply during integration.

Working together

Tackling the Real Issues

By Day One at the latest, functional and operational teams will have been exposed to the overall vision and objectives of the newly-formed organisation. The time has now come for them to translate these into practical plans for their specific part of the business. The new teams come together for the first time, staring with trepidation at a blank flipchart and, perhaps with suspicion at their new colleagues. Now what?

This is your first and best opportunity to begin directing them towards a new, common goal, and to give them the joint and individual responsibility for designing and implementing the plans that will bring about the espoused future. It is through the hard graft of strategy development, business planning, and new process design that new teams are forged. A sense of common purpose emerges and teams learn to be effective together. Starting with the original vision and high-level structure for the post-close business developed pre-close, each functional and operating team identifies their role and contribution to this vision, testing and refining the initial hypotheses and laying down the operating plans through which to execute the vision.

Operating model design and detailed planning are processes that truly help the new teams to meld together around a common goal. Teams should be given full autonomy to create their short and long-term objectives, define their organisational models, their business and integration plans, detailed activities and, of course, the associated capital and operating budgets.

As discussed in Chapter 5, post-close integration is a programme in which environments change, ambiguity abounds and flexibility is key. Counter-intuitively, this landscape also provides excellent opportunities for executive team building, an opportunity not to be missed. A new risk or discovery arises which threatens your plans? Get a joint team to work on a solution. An earlier operating model decision (e.g. around proposed organisational structure or IT system) now appears less appropriate? Pull together leaders from both sides to redesign the future. Need to explore new areas for value to compensate for fruit that simply becomes too hard to pick? Same answer. The fluidity of integration programmes means that people will have to think, create, communicate, design, plan and deliver 'on the fly'. Managed carefully, achieving group success through adversity will work wonders on your executive teams.

> **Creating a new executive team: Notes from the integration of Falconbridge Inc. into Xstrata Plc. – Claire Divver, former Group Director, Corporate Affairs, Xstrata**
>
> "At Xstrata, we acquired a new mining business in a commodity to which we had no exposure (nickel) and a set of capabilities we didn't possess, but knew we would require in the immediate future – large capital project development. We appointed the head of projects of the target company, Falconbridge, to run the new business, despite his lack of experience as a business

unit CEO. This was largely due to our belief in his capabilities and the cultural fit with Xstrata, but also his world-class project management skills. Alongside him, we assigned an existing Xstrata executive to guide him through the creation of a new business unit in the Xstrata mould and its integration into the overall Xstrata group.

From the first day we brought together the new business unit team to undertake a business planning exercise, starting at the top – with the vision, mission and principles of their new business. What would be their goals and objectives for the next year, five years and the longer term? What were the strategic issues the business faced: capital constraints, unacceptable returns on capital, construction of a new project, efficient expansion of an existing operation, the threat of new entrants from the East, and so on? What behaviours and values would they expect their employees to demonstrate and how were they to ensure they operated responsibly and safely?

Taking this team through these fundamental questions proved a very powerful way of melding the individuals into a group which tackled real, difficult issues, effectively co-opting them to take accountability for the solutions they themselves came up with. This was not a top-down imposition of solutions – not even of objectives. This was a team starting with a blank sheet of paper (literally) and forging their own future which, of course, they would be held accountable for delivering.

> The two constraints that we imposed from the corporate centre were the group values – these were non-negotiable and immutable – and the reporting requirements.
>
> The business unit values needed to reflect the group values, even if the emphasis was nuanced and more relevant to the business unit's culture and challenges.
>
> The reporting requirements from the business unit to the corporate centre were uniform across the group and reflected the monthly operating and financial metrics required to manage the group. The methodologies and systems for populating these reports, however, were not prescribed – operating teams were free to define their own approaches to measuring, collecting and analysing the data specific to their operations."

Cultural Differences: What to do?

Taking steps to build effective executive and leadership teams across the combined business is often overlooked as a solution to the infamous – and regularly misdiagnosed – issue in acquisition integration: cultural alignment. Sometimes organisations do have intractably incompatible cultures – behaviours, values, even underlying assumptions about the right way to conduct business professionally and ethically. If these values or fundamental beliefs of the organisation are not sufficiently overlapping, then perhaps the transaction should not have proceeded in the first place. There are times when

CEOs know instinctively that this is the case but choose to proceed with the combination regardless. In reality, though, no two organisations have perfectly coincident cultures and differences can often be overcome by creating a new, common culture based on important components of each organisation's values and principles.

Turning hated competitors into a strong team

An acquisition of a company with two manufacturing sites to form a new business unit rapidly became something the acquirer never expected. The two sites, themselves bought separately several years earlier, had been left to openly compete in the market for years. Added to this, a six-hour time difference, language and cultural challenges (former East German and Quebecois) had both sides accusing each other of gross incompetence and unethical behaviour...on Day One!

An exercise requiring them to work together to confirm and detail integration benefits, and to design the new business unit was just what was needed: supported by a formal assessment of values and organisational culture, a formal project mandating deep collaboration, joint workshopping, team building, and direct accountability for the end result turned two competitors into a unified, operationally-effective entity within a few short months.

While culture is often the lightning rod for blame in failed acquisitions, it still remains one of the most significant factors.

This is often because acquirers either dismiss it as 'too soft to be relevant' or 'too hard to be understood or solved', when it is in fact neither. The first and most important step is to start with a rational, realistic and objective view of whether you have a cultural difference that is likely to hinder the business, where in the organisation it is likely to cause you a problem, and what it looks like. There are as many cultural assessment tools and approaches as there are consultants implementing them. The key to selecting the right one is to make sure you understand up-front what you're trying to achieve, and how significant the challenge is that you face. If you take the simple view that culture is essentially 'the way we think, discuss and do things around here', then suddenly it doesn't sound like such a daunting challenge – find a new, common way of doing things, a set of principles and shared values which are acceptable to the vast majority and, in time, a new aligned culture will emerge.

Most of the time, there is sufficient common ground to move forward with some confidence without any structured efforts to assess and align cultures. Before diving into formal and extensive cultural assessment and alignment programmes, or worse, giving up on the acquisition as a lost cause, pause and take a step back. While fundamental differences in values and culture can be real and certainly derail acquisitions with frustrating regularity, often the real problem is simply that the various leadership teams within the new organisation don't have a shared vision of the future, don't share accountability for success with those on the 'other side', or may simply be 'storming' through the team building journey, not putting in the time to explore each other's fundamental beliefs as they relate to real decisions, real risks, real plans and real actions.

Can't we all just get along

The merger of Publicis and Omnicom was supposed to a combination of two equals, but the US and French media titans ended up calling it quits when cultural differences got in the way. Both CEOs wanted control and were unable to even get along for the sake of the deal.

Publicis did find harmony in its later acquisition of Sapient, a digital communications firm. Presented as the coming together of the old and the new, there were obvious differences in the styles and cultures of both companies. To address these differences, Publicis used the integration process as an opportunity to restructure around the innovative culture and capabilities Sapient could inject into the combined organisation and into the services provided to their customers. Sapient employees were empowered to be creative, but now had more and greater opportunities to take their ideas to the market.

So when people aren't getting along, make sure you understand the root cause of the disagreements before imposing what may be the entirely wrong solution. If the challenges remain more interpersonal in nature, look at ways to bring people together, the simplest of which is to get them working together, in the same place, on a common goal. Help them use the 'ladder of inference' and other techniques to ensure a common starting point from which consensus can be built. Use the team building approaches mentioned at the beginning of this chapter to help them 'form, storm, norm and perform' – a process that studies show must be restarted even if a single new individual joins an existing team.

Building the infrastructure

Getting accountability into the right hands

Just as building engagement and commitment to a goal is about ownership, team commitment – that is, commitment to a shared goal *and* to the team itself – can also be encouraged simply by setting clear, joint accountability for specific objectives. While those at the top – boards, CEOs, general managers – are clearly accountable for the final performance of the deal, elements of the integration must be delegated elsewhere, accompanied by sufficient delegated accountability.

Setting the right level of accountability at the start of integration design and planning is possibly the single most important driver of long-term M&A success. While an M&A team may have clear accountability for 'getting the deal over the line', clear accountability for delivering the *value* of the deal must simultaneously be 'baked into' the objectives of operational management – not a separate integration team. While such an integration project team can be central to co-ordinating and facilitating post-close success (e.g. through the provision of programme governance, project management structure and rigour, specialist expertise and additional resources), accountability and ownership for delivery of integration benefits must stay within line management responsible for the day-to-day running of the business – with one main exception: projects which cut across multiple business or operating units.

For every project within an integration programme, there should always be a sponsor within the business, a line manager with clear accountability – and the appropriate level of authority – to deliver the benefits of that project. For those projects that will be run entirely within one function or business unit, accountability naturally resides with the head of that function or business unit.

The difficulty inevitably comes when the project boundaries are not so clearly defined. Examples of such projects are many and varied: office relocations, creating a new business unit, closing a facility, disentangling business functions to work more autonomously. Here, objectivity is paramount. Consider the merging of two corporate headquarters: when accountability and authority falls to one of the two former group heads, decisions are likely to be made (or seen to be made) to 'their side's' advantage and the detriment of the other. Another often highly contentious situation can arise when shared costs need to be allocated across two or more operating units, for example when they share a common infrastructure or are located in the same operating environment.

The integration team can have a powerful role to play when you have a minimalist approach to corporate functions and you acquire a company with a large or even bloated corporate office. A novel approach to restructuring the corporate office is to create a 'free market' for the centralised functions, positions and even physical assets previously owned and managed by both legacy businesses. This is, in essence, a continuation of the accountability theme, where the operating unit and function heads are expected to define what they require from a central group, rather than having a new corporate group model imposed on them. This approach was very effectively applied by Xstrata, which had a very small corporate office in comparison with almost every company it acquired. In this case, the integration team would map out in detail the corporate functions, processes, roles and individuals of the acquired company and present this detailed map to the operating unit and corporate function heads in a meeting aimed at having each participant carve out the parts of the corporate function they required and were willing to take over. After some debate, what remained were the activities which were not seen as essential by either the operating or functional heads. The last step was to check these for redundancy with the existing corporate functions before eliminating unnecessary process at the corporate level. Naturally, a programme of separating the various components and devolving them to their new home – either a functional or operating unit – followed to ensure no disruption to day-to-day operations.

Such scenarios call for someone with a degree of separation from the immediate implications of such a decision, while still being close enough to the process to make a fully informed decision and to understand its impact. Ideally, the Integration Director should take on this responsibility or, failing this, a senior corporate executive – making the impartial decisions that are difficult to allocate elsewhere.

Monitoring and the executive board's role

While accountability for any integration project, function or business unit should rest with someone within the business, and preferably with the individual who will run the relevant function or business unit in the longer term, the progress of the major integration projects should be presented to and scrutinised by the executive committee or an equivalent group. Yet some of these projects can continue for some time, and at some point the board can start to feel pressed for time and other business priorities. The question is: When should

such board-level monitoring stop?

The answer is simple. Executive board-level oversight should continue until the final *acquisition* rationale and all associated benefits are delivered. By continuing to demonstrate executive interest in any such undertaking, momentum will be maintained and those in the business will know where their priorities should lie.

Reporting becomes less comprehensive as integration progresses. As individual projects are completed and their benefits delivered, status information on these projects will drop off the agenda, while the overall acquisition benefits and objectives continue to be monitored. Beyond this, the acquisition benefits should have been baked into the new business plans – for the company, the operating units and the various functions – setting in place a mechanism for continuous monitoring.

The tenure of the integration team

So we have a central integration team overseeing all the workstreams, reporting on costs, benefits and risks, and managing dependencies. For how long do we need them? Often referred to as an Integration Management Office, Integration Programme Office, or similar, this group (or individual) is important in 'oiling the wheels' of the programme, providing much-needed visibility of how all the moving pieces fit together, working to manage changes and conflict between workstreams and providing specialist skills, methods, tools and resources where needed across different functions as they integrate. So when should this group be disbanded? Simple: when they are no longer needed. Programme offices add value in situations in which risks and dependencies between and across functional and operating workstreams are high; once integration has progressed to a point at which these dependencies no longer exist, the need to manage them diminishes.

Another potential sign or trigger for diminishing the role of a central integration programme team is the finalisation of the business plans. Once a new functional or operational team is in place, objectives and actions are agreed and their business plan approved, the central integration team may be able to withdraw its services. Making this withdrawal explicit – at the Integration Steering Committee meeting or at the company's operating board – formalises the 'removal of the training wheels'. The managers of the operating team are still in the driver's seat (where they have always been) but are now on their own.

Our bias is towards transferring even the reporting activities from the integration process into the day-to-day agenda as quickly as possible. At this point, progress reports on outstanding integration activities relating solely to the function or business unit are no longer given to the Integration Steering Committee but are reported through the normal performance management structures and become part of the operating team's executive agenda.

Managing accountability: The role of consultants

The role of consultants in integration processes can be contentious. One often sees the entire integration – including accountability for benefits delivery – handed over to armies of consultants replete with methodologies, spreadsheets and tools, usually to the ultimate failure of the programme. This extensive use of consultants is often evident when the integration spans multiple countries, business units and products and the executive team is unsure of their own organisation's integration capabilities. What could be wrong with recruiting a firm which has performed multiple complex integrations to minimise the risk of failure? The answer is simple and should by now be clear – *loss of accountability*.

As we have belaboured, accountability is a key success factor in effective organisations. Dilution of the desire or ability of the business' employees to be accountable for their specific objectives can be the death knell of an organisation as its ability to perform, compete and adapt is eroded.

By and large, consultancies are (or should be) primarily motivated by two goals: being as helpful as possible to their clients and being seen to add value. However they may overestimate their experience and capabilities, leading to an unintended consequence: a tendency to take on as much accountability as possible. Placing consultants in a position where they can inadvertently or even actively usurp accountability can – despite the best of intentions to 'just help them get this done' – confuse accountabilities in the short-term. More damagingly, it can also delay the process of bedding down the organisation into a new, well-oiled business.

Consultants can play a positive role though, provided it is carefully defined and continuously measured against the criterion of accountability. In the best case, consultants have a cameo role aimed at bringing new, unique expertise to the integration process – e.g. in functional areas such as IT or HR, or cross-programme skills such as new process design, organisational design or change management and communications. Furthermore, an objective facilitator 'beholden to neither side', project manager, or simply an additional pair of analytical hands working alongside or for an employee can also prove helpful.

Consequently, there are two key criteria to apply when assessing the need to bring in a consultant or consulting firm. First, are they contributing a skill or resource that your organisation doesn't have and won't require into the longer term? Second, are their roles structured in a way that ensures they cannot remove or dilute the accountability of your managers?

On the first criterion there are inevitably a series of technical projects in any integration that require a certain skillset or level of manpower that a company should not be expected to hold in the normal course of business. Roles that are likely to be required over the longer terms should be filled, as soon as possible, by one of organisation's own employees, or recruited into a permanent position.

The second criterion demands that you appoint a consultant or firm that recognises the importance of internal accountability, and truly understands that their role should never allow the client to abrogate responsibility for running the business.

For a business that doesn't acquire or integrate regularly, or that is undertaking an unusual integration, there is a credible role for senior consulting support as a 'senior advisor' to the integration. This can be in a formal capacity as the group or individual responsible for tactically managing the Integration Programme Office, but never for the underlying integration deliverables and benefits. A consultant can add real value by bringing previous experience to the Integration Steering Committee, sitting on the shoulder of the Integration Director or helping to coach and mentor workstream leads. Provided the advisor doesn't become a crutch, this model capitalises on the consultant's experience, independence and objectivity without compromising internal accountability.

KEY CONCEPTS:

1. Build effective teams by having them work on real-live issues and challenges.

2. Emphasise the commonalities between the two companies' cultures and seek to create a new set of values and principles based on these commonalities.

3. Promote accountability relentlessly:

   a. Ensure the integration of all functions, operating units and projects are managed by a company executive;

   b. Continue monitoring all major projects and processes at the executive board level until their respective benefits are delivered;

   c. Ensure any cross-functional or cross-operating unit activities are managed by an objective executive, such as the Integration Director;

   d. Select any consultants and define their roles with an eye on maintaining accountability in the hands of your management in the short and longer term.

Chapter 7
COMMUNICATE, COMMUNICATE, LISTEN, COMMUNICATE

"Much unhappiness has come into the world because of bewilderment and things left unsaid."

FYODOR DOSTOYEVSKY

"The single biggest problem in communication is the illusion that it has taken place."

GEORGE BERNARD SHAW

"Finally, some progress, and results. With the help of his integration leaders, and with meticulous planning, Paul was now delivering a regular drip-feed of emails to all employees and customers letting them know how integration was progressing, what changes were upcoming and how it would impact them. Informally the word came back letting him know that the impact of these communications was immediate and positive – people were beginning to find some order in the uncertainty that surrounded them. Fear and doubt blown away by facts and data; works every time.

While this was all great, something still seemed to be missing.

*His team continued to see a lack of motivation within some
teams, and their employee turnover rate was still stuck at twice
the level it had been before the deal. They didn't seem to have
a handle on what people were actually thinking – no,* feeling
*– about the combined business. Paul realised that, while his
emails had perhaps settled the minds of his people, they hadn't
captured their hearts. Time to move his comms plan up a gear."*

Consistency: The importance of communication

If there is a single ingredient beyond accountability that
differentiates successful integrations from the pack, it is
the presence of high-quality, continuous and consistent
communication. Communication is recognised by all
executives as integral to leading any organisation and,
in particular, any change process. In the context of post-
merger or acquisition integration, communication takes on
an altogether more vital role, and a half-hearted attempt at
delivering key messages and progress updates is almost certain
to put the entire process at risk. Every single stakeholder
– internal and external – is unsettled by the change that
an acquisition or merger brings. As we have highlighted
earlier, in the absence of a compelling and continuous story,
individuals and groups will seek to fill the void with their own
narrative – often taking the form of inaccurate, negative and
unconstructive rumours. *Keep control of the narrative at all
times!*

Communication helps to build a sense of identity, can help people feel heard and more than anything else, helps to build and sustain the momentum that is so essential.

Surprisingly, though, it's rare to see communication of the quality essential for success. If you think at any time during integration that you may be over-communicating, think again in terms of breadth, messaging, understanding and feedback. Then communicate more, listen more, and share more. Obsess about communication.

Communication cannot be seen as a side-show, an adjunct or supporting function; it is central to every part of the integration process. From the time that detailed integration design commences, communication design and planning is a peer to the other operating and functional team analyses. Appoint a senior executive to lead it, someone with a seat on the Integration Steering Committee, to ensure both a proactive and holistic approach, but also to provide timely feedback at the highest level.

These two ingredients – *consistent* and *obsessive* communication – underpin any effective communications strategy. Consistent messaging means setting out the key messages of the integration process – including the desired benefits, key goals and expectations – and repeating them throughout, providing progress updates, highlighting successes that reflect these goals, and making positive examples of those individuals demonstrating the desired culture and values.

Obsessive communication is about being relentless, open and comprehensive, starting with the top of the organisation and working through all levels right through to the bottom. The communication strategy should ensure consistency and alignment across stakeholder groups and at each level of the organisation. The top executives must deliver the same messages to their lieutenants as they do on their roadshows to the various offices and operations. The lieutenants, in turn, must ensure their employees receive an appropriate, aligned version of the messages, while statements to external stakeholders – including investors – should be a tailored version of these same internal messages.

Communication is a line responsibility. While a communications team can help craft the key messages, prepare the material and monitor internal and external feedback – and even co-ordinate the overall activity – they cannot lead the exercise or give the communications themselves. Similarly, while PR teams and advisors have an important role to play in maintaining the messaging in the key channels, such as mainstream media and key influencers, it is the organisation's management who should set the agenda and, where feasible, deliver the messages. This places an extra burden on managers who are already stretched by their day jobs and the integration tasks that fall in their laps.

Consequently, those at the top must lead by example.

Given the challenges, it is no surprise that communication often falls by the wayside. It requires discipline and leadership to ensure the priority for this task is upheld.

Your communications goal

Designing a communications programme should be done with the intent of overcoming emotional barriers and gaining support, so pushing forward the agenda of integration as quickly as possible. While communicating is an essential tool in risk mitigation, it goes well beyond this by keeping support for the integration high at all times, by maintaining support for the changes, and so helping to sustain momentum. At its simplest, the integration communications plan should aim to do three things: stop the malicious spread of rumours by propagating the story you want to be heard; propel the integration forward by creating and spreading positive contagion (helping people feel part of a successful process); and help instill the values of your new company.

Control the narrative

The rumour mill is never more active than during a change programme. Speculation – 'water cooler talk' – is inevitable when things are up in the air, and this can't be helped. Rumours spread damaging stories that can weaken peoples' enthusiasm for change, or worse still, create fear and panic

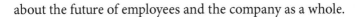

about the future of employees and the company as a whole.

Your first objective should be to project your predetermined narrative to fill any potential vacuum that would otherwise leave space for others to propagate their own stories.

Open, honest, respectful

The CEO of a listed natural resources company adopted an unusually-open communications strategy that immediately instilled a sense of trust and credibility. On meeting the acquired factory workers, he gave presentations covering why the company was bought, how much they spent to buy them, and the ROI needed to justify the purchase. He then went on to lay out initial thoughts on the future of the acquired unit, while stressing that he couldn't elaborate beyond that until they completed the necessary analysis and planning; a clear date was given for when this would be done and presented.

This same presentation was given to each and every shift in the factory, and any questions that couldn't be answered on the spot were followed up as soon as an answer became available.

Such an upfront approach allowed the company to immediately take control of the story, gain the trust and respect of employees and managers, and build their support for the work ahead of them.

You will never be able to respond to all uncertainties or concerns on Day One – but what you can do is provide a framework and a timeline by when answers will be given. If you can provide a definitive answer on the spot, do so. Think proactively about things that can be clarified, as trivial as they may seem to you. Deliver regular progress updates – especially against stated goals and performance targets.

Building trust requires consistency and integrity in communications. Detractors will be looking for inconsistencies between statements and actions. Communicate facts and delivered objectives, and always resist the temptation to project fanciful or wishful scenarios you think will placate your audience. As you repeatedly deliver what you set out to and communicate this, trust will gradually build, momentum will be created and a growing coalition of support will emerge. Communicate openly, including the mistakes or surprises. This will signal that you trust and respect your audience, earning their respect in return.

Leverage your momentum

Progress needs to be relayed again and again. News of successes – no matter how small – should be heard by those to whom they are relevant. Integration usually presents an uphill struggle to gain widespread support, and people need to believe that progress is being made and that they have backed the winning team. This is particularly important for the coalition of the willing – the small and hopefully growing pool of early adopters who amplify and project positive messages throughout the company and beyond. In the face of the inevitable resistance they will experience as the disciples of the integration, they will require the nourishment that success can provide to recommit to the process. Sceptics are more likely to get on board with your programme if you can convince them you can deliver what you said, and evidence is the most powerful persuader.

Creating and communicating *momentum* is therefore the next important objective. How to do this is of course up to you, but one obvious option is to simply broadcast it to the furthest corners of your organisation, leveraging today's technology and tools to best effect. Boring and long prose is no longer effective – video, live web-casts, short films and even cartoons can help deliver clear and powerful messages to invigorate stakeholders. In environments in which labour-dominated workforces are less familiar with the new digital world, industrial theatre which matches their cultural story-telling traditions can be very powerful.

As a serial acquirer, Xstrata constructed an integration website or portal for each transaction. This portal was a repository for information relating to every aspect of the integration, while importantly providing a facility for employees to privately post questions and provide feedback. On this portal, a weekly newsletter was published relaying the actions that had taken place that week – offices closed, new hires, new processes being rolled out, new contracts that were secured and so on. To populate this weekly update, every corner of the organisation would be scoured for examples of wins delivered over the past week, and by acknowledging the teams and individuals in question, a sense of momentum and energy was sustained.

Building a culture of positivity does not require waiting until a final goal has been delivered; in fact, it works the other way: it will be very hard to deliver your final goal without creating a positive mood first. Communicating smaller milestones along the way to your various objectives can build that sense of momentum. Instead of simply waiting until you're ready to move into the new office before revealing the news, provide updates along the way: we've identified five suitable locations; we've selected this one; we've finalised the lease arrangements; we've begun to fit-out the office; we've just had the office equipment delivered – all the way until the move date is official.

Embed your values as quickly and effectively as possible

Compromise and negotiation are a part of the process for nearly every element of an integration, with one big exception: the values you expect the new organisation to exhibit. As discussed in previous chapters, there are some values or aspects of your culture that are integral to the way you work and the success you've had so far. What served as the non-negotiables in your work pre-close should now be entrenched throughout the combined entity, helping consolidate a sense of shared identity.

It's best to embed these values as quickly as possible: you are creating a new organisation, and it's much easier to establish a unified set of behaviours, processes and culture at the beginning of an organisation's life than to wait until the organisation is bedded down.

Specific examples and careful language can have profound effects here, and senior executives must be aware of their responsibility to act as role models. The most effective method we've seen to disseminate the right values is to use your communications to highlight individuals and teams who have demonstrated the desired behaviours. Public recognition clearly and strongly broadcasts your expectations while also creating aspiration.

The essence of good communication is storytelling. Stories are useful constructs through which to communicate complex messages such as desired behaviours and demonstrate otherwise abstract or ambiguous values.

Driving cultural change at Xstrata – Claire Divver, former Group Director, Corporate Affairs, Xstrata

"The broader cultural scene-setting objective of our communications is partly done by the story of the company – Xstrata for example had a very strong creation story, which illustrated the type of company we were. Many companies have that type of narrative which is helpful to grab hold of, showing who the company is and where it has come from.

The management team is a particularly important figure in all of that – the communications from the chief executive need to have some examples of the values in action, showing how they get played out and what the company wants to see. As soon as we see examples of those values in the target company or integrated company it is important to highlight and celebrate them. So we try to amplify the good and set out some examples of employees doing things in the right way.

Beyond that, it is about living the values that you promote – throughout integration, the acquiring company is under the microscope just as much as the target company, so the entire management team needs to live the values and embody them.

For example, undergoing integration by changing everything on Day One was a great example of being agile and innovative. We also used to talk about being an empowering culture and wanting people to be accountable and responsible, so through our appointments we pushed decision-making down the organisation so that decisions were being made by the people with the best information."

At Xstrata, a section of the integration portal was used to post relevant stories featuring employees who had taken a specific action that was in keeping with one or more of the corporate values. These stories were carefully crafted in an engaging and celebratory style and included vivid imagery aimed at reinforcing the selected messaging. Over time, a repository of these stories from across the globe emerged and rolling stories were ultimately published on the corporate website, surviving the integration and visible to internal and external stakeholders. For example, if you place a high value on innovation, an employee using a novel solution to repair a broken piece of equipment could form the core of one of these stories. If you value environmental sustainability, a story about an individual finding a better type of grass to rehabilitate an old industrial site can suitably communicate what's expected.

Communication essentials

Listen, listen, listen

Communication cannot simply involve the broadcasting and dissemination of information.

Listening helps people feel that they have a voice and that they are important to the process. Beyond this, listening is essential in making sure you find out early when things are going wrong and, in this sense, is a central input into managing your risks. Listen out for staff discontent and any critical issues they bring to your attention; for anxiety among your customers (fed perhaps by your competitors); for concerns from governmental bodies and trade unions; and from all other groups.

An effective communications strategy should also feed back directly to those leading the various integration initiatives. A feedback page on the integration portal, a confidential e-mail facility, regular facilitated meetings with small groups to gauge the temperature, exit interviews – all these techniques and more are key to keeping a finger on the pulse, while also developing a sense of involvement. Nothing is more debilitating than feeling unheard – and helplessness is a recipe for dissatisfaction and, in time, dissent. The simple act of soliciting questions on an integration portal – visible only to the Integration Director, for example – and crafting pubic responses to the most prominent queries and anxieties, while addressing the most pressing private ones directly, can bring people 'into the tent', while providing valuable proactive intelligence to the integration and business leadership.

Sophisticated social media analytics tools can provide insight into the narrative taking place in the public domain – often contributed to by employees, but also by third parties. Online or facilitated surveys can reach large groups in a confidential manner, while focus groups are helpful in soliciting the thoughts of small teams. Key influencers are often recipients of information from those who respect them and, if they're willing and it's done in an open, ethical way, can be co-opted into the intelligence gathering exercise.

A proper communications exercise should be as participatory as possible. Build in feedback loops to assess understanding and buy-in; and act upon them to reinforce positive messages and to take the initiative when red flags start waving.

Assessing your communications

Each company has its own way of communicating, and many have robust and sophisticated processes and protocols to support an integration without reinventing the wheel. Nevertheless, it can still be helpful to assess the profile and range of your individual communications 'products' using the simple matrix below:

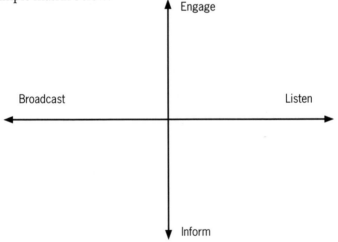

The horizontal axis plots the extent to which your communications 'product' is simply broadcasting messages without giving the recipient a direct opportunity to respond (e.g. email, posters); or conversely whether you are using this communication to listen to the concerns, suggestions and complaints of your stakeholders. The vertical axis reflects the intent of your communication product: is it simply designed to inform your stakeholders of new facts or data (e.g. the go-live of a new system or the appointment of a new manager), or is it helping to motivate and help them along the change curve?

This matrix is a simple way to test the breadth of your communication activities. A broad spectrum of communication techniques does not necessarily translate into a strategy that achieves the range of objectives that that your communications has set out to deliver, but it will help you ensure that you're covering all the bases, both intellectually and emotionally. Regularly plotting the various communications activities underway throughout the integration on this simple matrix will help you hone in on what your communications approach may be missing, allowing you to maintain the right balance, and ensuring your communications strategy is complete and holistic.

Assessing through middle management: the sponge layer – Claire Divver, former Group Director, Corporate Affairs, Xstrata

"In integrations, it is middle management who typically disseminate the culture throughout the company. Often when communications comes down from the top and feedback comes from the bottom, if you're not careful both can just get absorbed by the middle management layer and go no further. It's important to work closely with middle management to understand what's going on with them, and to support them. Often they will be conveying messages they themselves don't necessarily buy into.

It's a common mistake to forget the middle managers are employees too. Asking people straight off the bat to be leaders in a new business without the background, understanding and buy-in of what they're being asked to communicate is a very big ask.

Supporting them requires that you provide better toolkits to equip middle managers. Give them dedicated training sessions, so that you can understand their own concerns and questions, and set out your expectations for them to help cascade messages and lead the workforce."

Get out in front

Senior executives can have a tendency to hide during an integration. Their workload increases exponentially and their visibility tends to fall just at the time when it should increase. All senior executives know that leadership involves regular communications. During integration however, this requirement is more acute, and executive absence is quickly spotted and likely to inadvertently deliver unsettling messages.

Senior executives need to be visible to employees and stakeholders at all times. Bringing authority, accountability and respect to centre-stage, their presence demonstrates senior buy-in and makes it easier to carry others along with them.

For single-location companies this is, of course, easier. While the logistics for businesses spanning multiple locations becomes slightly trickier, heightened visibility should still be expected of both business unit and group executives. While this probably necessitates even more time-consuming travel, the judicious use of digital tools can help leverage their time more effectively.

Coordinating this effort requires requires detailed planning, organisation and no small amount of cajoling. The CEO and the Integration Director need to encourage other senior executives to ensure they have covered the bases and that they're sending the right positive message.

Executive 'town hall' communications come in many forms from physical meetings and business unit visits to video presentations or even voicemail broadcasts. All of these should be repeated across multiple groups and locations depending on the scale of your operations. This task has been made easier by technology, making it possible to broadcast meetings while providing the facilities to ask questions remotely. However, this shouldn't prevent you from being present whenever possible – clever technology doesn't absolve you of the need to maintain sufficient physical presence. Non-virtual communications are more personal, direct and interactive, allowing the senior executive to communicate not only momentum, but also the values, what they are expecting to happen and so on; it is also much easier to listen, and listen more effectively, in person. As a rule of thumb the CEO, CFO and Integration Director should all visit the major geographies within six weeks of Day One.

KEY CONCEPTS:

1. Make communications and the communications executive an equal partner in the integration process.

2. Be consistent and obsessive when communicating to all stakeholders.

3. Ensure communications is a line responsibility. Require all managers to play their part in relaying messages to employees and other stakeholders, and train and support them in this role.

4. Use communications to:

   a. Keep control of the narrative at all times;

   b. Create and support momentum;

   c. Embed your values throughout the organisation.

5. Make communications bidirectional to:

   a. Allow your employees and other stakeholders to feel heard;

   b. Help keep your ear close to the ground.

6. Ensure senior management maintain a high level of visibility throughout the integration process, not just at the start.

Chapter 8
STAY THE COURSE THROUGH MEASUREMENT

"Measurement is the first step that leads to control and eventually to improvement. If you can't measure something, you can't understand it. If you can't understand it, you can't control it. If you can't control it, you can't improve it."

H. JAMES HARRINGTON

"At last, 12 months post-close, Paul got his holiday: two weeks in the Seychelles, far, far away from risk logs, dashboards, employee pulse surveys, screaming executives and disinterested board members. Labelled a qualified success by almost all objective observers, Paul simply felt glad it was over.

Then the inevitable email arrived: "Given the many ups and downs of this deal since last summer, could Paul prepare an assessment of the overall success of the acquisition to present to the board two days after his return from holiday?"

Setting aside his frustration at the timing, Paul had another problem. As one would expect when reflecting on an integration process, some of the benefit streams were 'green stars' – over-

delivering on time and in some cases under budget: while others were 'red dogs' – never really achieving what they set out to do. Everyone already knew this deal ended up as a bit of a mixed bag, that was no surprise. The real issue was that Paul realised he had absolutely no idea why the 'green' ones were green, and why the 'red' ones were red.

But this time, Paul had a plan. He knew his formal 'integration reboot' six months ago had created a much better connection between deal benefits, integration objectives and specific workstream deliverables. This in turn delivered a heightened sense of personal accountability for success, and vastly improved communications. Measurement of programme delivery and business performance had ratcheted up a gear once his executive team finally accepted responsibility for delivering the deal business case. The data was there and was not disputed, irrespective of whether it pointed to a positive or less successful outcome. It just needed analysing. Time to get his team working while he enjoyed the last few days of his break..."

Most managers – especially those with a finance or engineering bent – will tell you that measuring and monitoring key metrics is essential in business and that this is no less important for each and every stage of integration. In their most obvious guise, metrics help you know how integration is progressing, when it is going off course, and where changes need to be made. In the context of an integration process, metrics can also indicate when reporting on an activity or workstream should transition from the integration team into business as usual – in other words, when formal integration support can end for a particular initiative. Indeed, most companies would commonly apply many of the same metrics to an integration project as they do in their day-to-day business, albeit with greater focus and more frequent monitoring.

At this point, you may be thinking that this is all self-evident. As a senior executive, the importance of metrics and performance management has probably been drummed into you since the first day you stepped into your first job. What isn't always appreciated is the impact metrics have on the psychology of people leading, and experiencing, change and integration. Remember, metrics drive behaviour. While most recognise their power to build and sustain momentum, and to drive leadership focus and attention in everyday business, this power is rarely applied to an integration process to anywhere near the same degree. More powerful still, using metrics to refine your M&A strategy once the deal and integration are over and done will help drive your company's long-term behaviours; those very behaviours we've been stressing in every previous chapter of this book. It will continuously improve your company's approach to acquisition (from target selection through deal completion), and help you develop deep institutional capacity for delivering successful integrations – a potent source of competitive advantage for serial acquirers.

We need to reimagine the importance and use of metrics in integration processes. Metrics are not just there to let you know when you've achieved your goal. Nor are they simply early-warning indicators of when the process is becoming derailed – although this is important. Metrics provide tangible, actionable information during a time of great uncertainty. Using metrics in your communications with employees and other stakeholders can act as a calming force, putting concrete, objective facts against goals and objectives when everything around them can seem overwhelming, emotionally-charged and largely intangible.

Metrics should be thought of as a series of signposts lighting all the available paths you might take along your journey. Any experienced integration practitioner will tell you that post-deal integrations are the most entrepreneurial activities an organisation can undertake. Things are not always what they seemed when detailed integration design was completed what now seems so very long ago. Corrective or opportunistic decisions have to be made on the fly and with some regularity. For this reason, within an integration programme, metrics are the tool that enables *responsible agility*, aiding effective, rapid but risk-aware decision-making. For every metric that you think of, you need to know ahead of time what you would do in each possible scenario when the metric flashes green, amber or red. Being armed with these contingencies and the relevant limits that trigger alternative courses of action is central to making a higher number of correct decisions at speed and under pressure. Applying a more traditional approach to metrics, you can find yourself measuring things because you know they are important. However, if you would take the same course of action regardless of what the measurement is telling you, then the metric is redundant – of no use to you or the integration programme.

Momentum is sustained by being able to take quick and often, proactive, action. People will continue to feel they're in good hands as the organisation uses integration metrics to demonstrate its ability to be decisive and responsive during the storm, keeping the show on the road despite the buffeting winds of change. Furthermore, reporting the relevant metrics to senior executives and the board will ensure that those accountable for that metric will stay focused and attentive. Finally, a proactive facility with the appropriate metrics can and should feed into your growing institutional memory, making future integrations smoother as patterns of recognition develop across an increasingly broad set of eventualities.

Recognising all of this, the biggest challenge comes in selecting and designing the right metrics, then using them to feed your current and future integrations. Here's how you do it.

Don't just follow the money

'What gets measured gets managed' is a prevailing theme through most companies. Yet while the signposting potential of metrics is accepted, many organisations fail to make it an integral part of their integration practice. For many, metrics are the only visible face of the business, with overall financial (and asset) performance taking centre-stage. This behavioural bias stems from another truism – 'what worries the board gets measured'.

The problem is that many of these measures are either backward-looking or don't bring about a change in direction, priority or behaviour. Growth in revenue, profit, return on equity or other financial metrics are important, of course, and pleasing if they are moving in the right direction over the course of an integration. On their own, however, they can provide a simplistic picture of how the business – and the deal – are doing post-close across a broader set of dimensions as the integration unfolds. How is employee engagement? Or safety? Or customer perception, acquisition or churn? What about product quality or dropped service calls? Are noise-related community complaints increasing, or environmental incidents?

Focusing on higher-level lagging indicators can cause you to fail to see issues as they start to appear, and to miss your opportunity to intervene. Once a lagging indicator signals that all is not well, you may have lost the momentum you worked so hard to foster, forcing you to run harder to get back to where you started. Remember, when large and complex programmes (including integrations) fail, they rarely do so because of a single catastrophic event. More commonly they fail due to a 'snowballing' of minor problems that go unseen or unaddressed, which then accumulate, accelerate, and eventually overwhelm.

Go above and beyond – or rather, below and ahead of – traditional financial metrics. Your integration plans identified synergies and opportunities for value creation which, while aimed at improving the long-term financial health of the combined organisation, were defined to include a broad and varied range of sub-targets: customers, suppliers, costs, office headcount, units produced, brand recognition, safety performance, capital productivity, new customers acquired, revenue per customer, quality of R&D pipeline – the list goes on. While still being focused on the overall objectives of the deal and the specifics of your business, these metrics should be as leading in their nature as possible. They should help you predict future outcomes, not just look back on past ones. You will need a balanced scorecard of these deal and integration-related objectives alongside those used for your day-to-day business. The good news is that the groundwork will have been laid during detailed transaction and integration design. In fact, these leading metrics should have been agreed up-front, pre-close.

The first set of measurements we use are by their nature derived from (or simply are) the acquisition benefits you identified when weighing up the deal. From these high-level benefit targets, a number of underpinning goals and interim or sub-targets should cascade. From these, you can pick and choose the most appropriate things to measure. The challenge is not only recognising what best indicates when you've achieved your final result – which will often be a financial measurement – but also disentangling the complex web of inputs and interactions that may have led to this.

A second set of measurements should be based specifically on your integration plan. You need to monitor progress against specific, often qualitative, project and programme milestones that you've set out. This is standard progress measurement, checking these goals against your timeline. Have you combined your operational structures? Have you rebranded the merged entity? Have you harmonised the policies and standards of your risk management team? Is the combined payroll system in place?

The third set of metrics uses a subset of your own standard operating metrics to see if you're affecting the underlying business as your integration progresses. This is a necessary health check and you don't need to reinvent the wheel. Unless the acquisition drastically changes the underlying business, you can use ongoing KPIs that talk to business performance and fulfilment capability, focusing on anything that might be adversely impacted or derailed by an integration programme. Examples include your safety performance, customer service, absenteeism, quality of manufacturing, investor relations and so on. Simply monitor these metrics a bit more closely than you normally would, setting specific, tighter than normal tolerances to identify any red flags early.

The fourth and final set of metrics we suggest relates to employee morale. Irrespective of your preferred method – surveys, questionnaires, pulse checks etc. – you need to make sure you can tap into how people are feeling about the deal, integration and consequent changes. Data gathered and the insights they provide can help you determine the pace at which your staff are advancing along the change-curve, how much progress they think you're making in achieving integration goals and whether there are any serious obstacles heading in your direction. Opinion is a rich source of information and insight – use it!

Collecting data from these four groups of metrics should reflect exactly what the executive committee cares about and serve to alert those in the business of these priorities. This helps to align focus at all levels of the organisation as it becomes clearer to employees how their actions contribute to executive priorities.

Get behind the numbers

Challenging though it may be, it is important that you quantify and time-define your metrics. As the acronym goes, make them SMART. Financial metrics normally spring to mind, but with a bit of thought, most other things can be quantified, measured and monitored, even if sometimes indirectly.

Take one simple example: your sales have remained steady, but can you infer from this that customers haven't felt the changes going on? Particularly for niche or business-to-business sales, a negative impact on sales may take some time to become evident as buyers will take longer to find a new supplier or contracts take time to unwind. By this point it may be too late. What's more, it could well have been preventable if only you had known about the problem earlier. If, in addition to sales, you monitored and reported the quality of production, frequency of faulty products, service measures such as customer response time, or other quantifiable component metrics, you may realise that a fundamental part of your business is underperforming – before the customer takes action.

Simpler still, you could ask your customers for feedback. Far from burdening your customers, seeking their input – especially in a B2B environment – can not only provide some early warning indicators of the health of your customer relationships and the activities of your competitors, but may well strengthen your relationships by virtue of them feeling included in your change process.

Quantification allows you to set clear targets and tolerance levels, which in turn help to detail your intervention plan. Take employee engagement: you may determine for a specific integration that the best you can expect in this case is for people to feel neutral about working in the new organisation. Set your limits at, for example, 70% or more employees feeling neutral towards the company as green, 50% as amber and 40% as red. When 70% of people are responding positively or neutrally, carry on as normal. Beneath 70%, dig into the data and perhaps hold some additional employee focus groups to better understand the situation. Beneath 50% and your contingency intervention kicks in.

All metrics in the 'green' zone over a sustained period may in itself constitute a warning sign. Rarely do integrations run universally smoothly, and such results can suggest either that you've chosen the wrong metrics or that they're not being reported accurately.

Politics and ownership

Existing data is collected from the department that usually owns the particular metric that interests you, and new metrics you've set up tend to be collected by the integration team.

Once collected, the metrics are collated and presented as a dashboard to the executive committee overseeing the entire integration, with each different workstream or department highlighted and metrics presented in the form of a traffic light system (green, amber or red).

The purpose of this is, of course, to help track the progress of the integration, while highlighting any potential areas of concern, allowing the executive committee to recognise where more resources or a change of plan is needed. The danger, as mentioned above, is that when people realise that their workstream may be reported as amber or red, the temptation will exist for owners to 'qualify away' or hide this information, discredit the messenger (typically the Integration Programme Director), and attempt to redeem the situation independently.

These defensive behaviours can be mitigated by building trust and relationships with the workstream owners, helping them understand why the accurate reporting of all integration metrics is important, even if in this case is presents their area in a bad light. When taking on the job, everyone must understand and accept that monitoring of progress will only improve the overall chance of success if conducted without fear or favour, which is ultimately in everyone's interest. Importantly, they need to see this process as a proactive approach to helping them succeed through the relevant allocation of resources. Amber exists as a 'minor warning', allowing people to signal that things are not progressing as planned and that some form of remedial action may be required. In keeping with the building of trust, the decision on whether to act and in what form should be informed by the workstream leader and taken jointly with the executive committee.

When should you act? The first thing to do is look at the integration holistically – how does this project or metric feed into the integration overall? To what degree will missing this lower-level milestone impact the higher-level benefit? As with any large and complex project, there are likely to be a web of interdependent tasks, decisions and milestones in your integration. Classic project management concepts of critical path, slack and resource levelling are therefore likely to come into play.

In the end, what does success look like?

The work is done, the teams have been disbanded and everyone is in their 'everyday' role. The last thing anyone feels like doing is conducting a thorough review of how the programme went and the degree to which it met the original acquisition objectives. But this is *precisely* what needs to be done, before it's too late, memories have faded, revisionist history takes root, or you are in the throes of your next transaction. For what purpose and on what basis should you conduct this review?

Naturally, each transaction has its own idiosyncratic objectives beyond improving the long-term value of the business. In general, the logic of an acquisition is based on inter-asset synergies expected to arise when the merged or aligned organisations can support activities more profitably in combination than they could separately. Furthermore, beyond economies of scale or scope, the acquirer may be pursuing access to new markets, customers, products or geographies or, in keeping with the resource-based approach, the acquisition of new capabilities or prize industry assets. Any of these motivations – if achieved – can result in a change in the acquirer's strategic position within its market. For serial acquirers in a consolidating industry, it may even change the overarching structure of the sector itself.

Given this, we can look in three broad areas for clues of how successful a transaction is in the long-term.

First, **strategic positioning**: has the deal supported your long-term strategy? The most relevant metrics here are the non-financial goals that you've been monitoring throughout. On top of this, try to ascertain whether relevant capabilities were added to the business, the strength of the senior management team and the reaction of investors.

Second, **financial returns**: is your business financially stronger, currently and into the future? Overarching profitability goals, such as revenue, EBITDA, net profit margin, ROCE, EPS etc. rightly tend to take centre-stage here. But measuring the financial strength of a company should also look at the extent to which other financial metrics have been optimised. Has the cost of capital reduced? Have you optimised your tax structure? What is the longer-term profitability potential following the new acquisition?

Finally, **operations post-close**: have you delivered a more efficient and effective business? Looking holistically at the business, have synergies been achieved without a greater cost being incurred? When considering this final element, the opinion and morale of customers and employees needs to be analysed alongside operational efficiencies and revenue growth. For example, if you've completed one or two deals and your SG&A expense ratio has increased, this is cause for concern, regardless of whether costs elsewhere have improved.

The requisite data needed to conduct a post-deal review already exist, having been actively collected throughout the integration – keep them and add them to those from previous deals to develop a long-term view of your M&A performance across multiple deals. Our own research[1] has shown that only 54% of acquirers regularly conduct formal reviews to measure M&A success. Learning from past mistakes is the only way to improve the execution success of your M&A strategy.

Used properly, metrics therefore can, and should, be the source that feeds a learning culture within your organisation.

1: Inconvenient Truths (Beyond the Deal LLP, 2017)

Beyond the Deal M&A Performance Index

Does your M&A support your mid- and long-term strategy?

- **Executive Tenure:** Does the board believe in a proven strategy and the leadership's ability to execute?
- **Transaction Beta:** Do investors recognise the performance of the transactions made?
- **P/E Ratio:** Do analysts value the future?

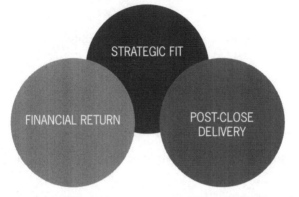

Is the business financially stronger?

- **Net Profit Margin:** Is the buisness more cash-generative?
- **Return on Equity:** Is it generating a better return on its capital?
- **EPS Growth:** Does your M&A help you return more to investors?

Have your deals delivered a more efficient, effective buisness?

- **Sales Growth Rate:** Have your acquisitions accelerated revenue growth?
- **SG&A%:** Is your back-office more efficient?
- **Net Income/Employee:** Are your people more focussed and effective?

When reviewing performance, never sweep mistakes under the rug and just hope they won't happen again. Rather, focus on them and extract the necessary learnings for improvement. By doing so, you'll advance an environment ripe for learning, and create a systemic, institutional capability within your organisation to deliver value from your M&A strategy, deal after deal.

Institutionalise best practice M&A and integration capabilities

Once the work of integration is truly over, those with aspirations to become a serial acquirer should be thinking "How do I ensure the process goes more smoothly the next time"?

Being a consummate integrator is a source of competitive advantage for a serial acquirer – because you can get back to pursuing the next transaction in short order and your underlying organisation is ready to take on another target. If you can do this more quickly and successfully than your competitors, you can win the consolidation game.

The best serial acquirers – such as CISCO, Oracle, PVH, Koc and Xstrata – have institutionalised approaches and well-formed know-how for M&A and post-deal integration. Furthermore, they have developed networks of individuals within their organisations who have conducted numerous M&A processes and can get back on-board quickly to effectively lead integration exercises. Such companies have processes and principles they apply across all their M&A campaigns and, most importantly, they continually and proactively refine their tradecraft.

Despite every transaction having unique characteristics, the completion of each deal presents an opportunity to reflect on the fundamental principles and specific techniques applied to integration, so that you can continually hone the processes and skills ahead of the next transaction. What did you do well? What caused problems? What would you change next time round? Did we learn something this time that could constitute a best practice for our developing tradecraft?

This integration tradecraft includes the templates, process maps, team structures and other documentation that reflects your deepening knowledge-base. Increasingly, companies are creating electronic repositories from which future M&A teams can draw to get up the learning curve more quickly. Web or cloud-based repositories are becoming more common, providing access to teams across the globe. To capture the less tangible aspect of your emerging best practice – including much of what we've discussed in this and previous chapters – how-to videos and stories told by the most experienced practitioners on specific aspects of the process are an easy way to share learning, as are well-constructed case studies.

KEY CONCEPTS:

1   Measuring and monitoring key metrics is essential in business but never more so than at each stage of a post-deal integration process.

2   Metrics should be thought of as a series of signposts showing the available paths at key times in the process.

3   Remember to quantify and time-bound each of your metrics, and to assign them clear, individual ownership.

4   Three areas that can be used to judge the long-term success of a transaction are: strategic positioning; financial returns; and operations post-close.

Chapter 9:
WHEN ALL IS SAID AND DONE

Acquisitions and mergers are here to stay. They are a permanent and important component of any executive team's strategic armoury. But our track record is poor at best. Like it or not, we have to become better at integrating the businesses we buy.

The management science behind post-transaction integration has come a long way over the past two decades. Frameworks, blueprints, project plans and practitioners now abound. Yet this has not moved the needle sufficiently. Something appears to be missing from the tradecraft – an element altogether more elusive and less obvious than the 'hard' methodologies which are now well understood. In this book, we have sought to shed some light on this apparently intangible ingredient – or set of ingredients – by highlighting some of the key areas of leverage or intervention for senior executives. Indeed, it is the very attitudes and behaviours of senior executives which make the difference between success and various degrees of failure. This book aims to guide the leadership-focused actions which distinguish successful acquirers.

Worth repeating are the key principles that run through every aspect of successful integration processes:

- *Accountability*: Keep accountability clear – single point, bright-light scrutiny with consequences for the outcome;

- *Balancing Opportunity and Risk:* Integration is the balance of risk and opportunity. Both are present in abundance – ensure you have identified and designed activities to deal with both;

- *Building and Sustaining Momentum:* Any transformation programme requires uninterrupted momentum to ensure the end-point is reached. This is a leadership responsibility;

- *Visible Leadership:* Be much more visible than ever. Your actions will guide the behaviours of others;

- *Focusing on the 'me' issues:* All stakeholders will be asking what the process and its outcome means to them. Until this single question has received sufficient attention for all key actors, real progress is unlikely;

- *Communicating Bidirectionally:* Regular, tailored and multifarious communication is the lifeblood of successful transformations and underpins the creation of momentum, building of trust, pre-emptive sourcing of critical information and cultural shaping; and

- *Measuring what is to be Managed:* Metrics are central to any scientific management endeavour – and no less so for complex integration processes.

One of the factors that provide an indication of future success is how early you begin the integration work. Waiting for the transaction to close is a sure-fire way of courting failure. Integration design is not only an integral part of transaction due diligence, but it should inform the transaction valuation and terms, and sometimes even the transaction itself. Part of integration due diligence should help you understand the inevitable cultural divides and commonalities. Assuming these will sort themselves out is, frankly, naïve and can jeopardise the transaction and the value it is meant to deliver. Assessing culture goes hand-in-hand with having a clear view of what makes your organisation successful and how much of this you see as crucial to the success of the combined entity. Don't compromise on these factors.

The integration team cannot be made up of those who are currently underemployed or between roles. Only the A-team will do, led by an Integration Director for whom you have big plans. Only the best team can manage the leadership nuances and inevitable surprises that characterise integration processes. Oh, and please don't appoint your best team and then dilute or confuse their accountability. Let them get on with the work with all the clarity and authority required by top performers.

The pre-close period is pivotal in many ways. Developing a healthy and accurate view of the other company and how it actually operates is fundamental to engender confidence on both sides – confidence that the integration teams knows what they're doing. This goes hand-in-hand with a clear and compelling vision of the future combined entity, and will reduce resistance and allow positive momentum to develop.

Along with the acquisition itself, your transaction will also buy you a licence for change, but one that carries with it a short shelf life. This is a valuable gift not to be squandered. Move quickly to signal that change is indeed underway and that the inevitable pain is likely to lead to a brighter future – for individuals, not just the business – before too long. The alternative – to step gingerly through transformation – will result in the re-ossification of the organisation, a state increasingly impossible to prise open as time goes on.

The enthusiasm of deal-doing often causes us to ignore the risks. Even if we seek to understand them, we often make the assumption that they are unlikely to come to pass, as we prefer to focus on the far more pleasant opportunities the combination promises. Risk and opportunity exist in equal measure when integrating two organisations. Identifying risks and designing detailed mitigation and avoidance plans permits you to pursue the opportunities with greater confidence and fervour.

Integration teams – even the best ones – become overwhelmed at some point in the process. They need a way to prioritise their decisions and the allocation of scarce resources. The sources of value and risk already identified offer the perfect yardsticks against which to prioritise – something that needs to be done objectively, ruthlessly and relentlessly. There is always time to return to less important activities, but it can be too late to realise a significant opportunity that has gone to a competitor or to mitigate a disastrous risk that wasn't addressed when it first arose.

Throughout the transaction and, subsequently, integration, it is teams of people which bring about the change and start the organisation on its new journey. The combined entity will comprise new teams at all levels, with new mandates and objectives. Being adept at building these effective teams quickly can become a source of advantage – especially for serial acquirers – and help move the organisation towards its new goals, while quickly preparing it for the next large initiative, even a new transaction.

All executives know the importance of communication. What few anticipate, though, is the degree to which the need for regular communication with (not just to) all groups takes on a completely new dimension in transformation processes like post-transaction integration. Everyone is responsible for communications – but none more than the line managers. Communicate constantly, clearly and bidirectionally.

"What can't be measured can't be managed." Every cliché holds a grain of truth, and this one has more than most. The integration itself and what it achieves must be monitored, compared against expectations and adjusted to stay on course.

Metrics will inform senior management when the work is done and business-as-usual can resume in each function or business area.

Good acquirers and integrators incorporate many of the elements highlighted in this book.

Excellent acquirers and integrators however, go one step further. Once the work is done, they have the discipline to revisit their programme, reflect on its successes and failings, and extract the learning; no matter how painful, tedious or obvious it may seem. They incorporate the key insights into their tradecraft, which becomes institutionalised as a body of knowledge available to the next team tasked with conducting a transaction or integration. This allows them to approach deals with confidence and so get ahead of their competition. They quickly put their organisations into steady-state after a transaction, capturing the deal benefits early and pre-empting their competitors for the next opportunity.

Finally, we close by pointing out that, while the principles addressed in this book have been discussed in the context of post-transaction integration many are common to transformation programmes of all types and have been applied in whole or in part in restructuring or transforming organisations outside the scenario of an immediate merger or acquisition. Whether the transformation aims to reduce costs, change organisational models, pursue new markets or bring about a cultural change, the key leverage points dealt with here are equally valid – as are many of the tools embedded within every step of the integration process. Organisational and cultural reviews, risk assessment and mitigation plans, selecting the A-team, maintaining momentum through leadership, communicating relentlessly through the line, creating effective teams, defining and monitoring key metrics, concentrating accountability, focusing on 'me' issues, prioritising against risk and opportunity and so on – all these have a central role to play in any change programme. We can confidently draw from this toolbox when designing, planning and executing any transformative programme, be it a restructuring, outsourcing, business unit shut-down, or other.

Like you, we are practitioners. Through this book, we have aimed to 'fill in the white space' on the integration programme plan with what we consider, based on our experience, to be the 'secret sauce' that typically means the difference between a failed acquisition and those we have seen that regularly, objectively beat expectations in delivering stakeholder value. With each passing transaction our tradecraft is constantly developing too and, in this spirit, we invite you and other practitioners to share your own insights on our LinkedIn discussion group: Leading the Deal. In time, the general body of knowledge will mature and, we hope eventually, the performance and pain of integration will cease to be a topic of debate and anxiety in boardrooms.

Thras is an executive at SuSeWi, a company producing algae as a protein alternative for fish feed and other applications.

Thras Moraitis was a cofounder and partner at X2 Resources – a $4bn natural resource-focused private investment vehicle – responsible for strategic development, investor management, communications and post-acquisition integration.

Prior to this, Thras was Group Head of Strategy and Corporate Affairs and a member of the Executive Committee at Xstrata plc until the company was sold to Glencore in 2013.

Over the past three decades, Thras has been involved in tens of transactions totalling over $50bn – as a principal investor, an advisor to major multinationals and as a public company C-suite executive.

Over his career, Thras has travelled to some sixty countries, lived in four and worked in over thirty.

Thras has authored various articles on strategy, leadership development and M&A. He co-wrote the book "Playing at Acquisitions", Smit and Moraitis, Princeton University Press, 2015, and authored related articles published in Long Range Planning and California Management Review.

Thras is married, has two children and lives in London.

Carlos Keener is an M&A and integration specialist and Founding Partner of Beyond the Deal (BTD), a full life-cycle M&A, integration and separation consultancy with a track record of helping clients deliver long term value 'beyond the deal' for more than 100 clients around the  world. He brings twenty years of international M&A, organisational change and project management experience across a variety of sectors including pharmaceuticals, retail, FMCG, media, oil & gas and natural resources.

Since establishing BTD in 2001, Carlos has advised dozens of organisations including Coca-Cola, E.On, Centrica, Unilever, Xstrata and EMI. Major deals in which he was involved include the merger of Glaxo Wellcome and SmithKline Beecham in 2001, the acquisition of Corus by Tata Steel in 2007, and the merger of bwin and PartyGaming in 2011.

Carlos is also a Non-Executive Director for a US/Egyptian business in the oil and gas sector. Carlos has a wife and two children, and lives in London.

INDEX

ABC 99

ability to accommodate new
    acquisition 39

accountability 20, 54, 178–81, 227
    dilution of 53, 227
    embedding 35
    consultants 54–5
    risk management 154, 156, 159,
      160–1, 164
    role of consultants 184–6
    setting right level 178
    value of 52

asymmetric insight 84–5

balancing opportunity and risk 20–1,
    226

branding change 101

building and sustaining momentum
    21, 224
    see also momentum

business plan, finalisation 183

BWIN 96

Cadbury 43, 122

change
    confidence in presenting change
      80, 83
    curve 75
    managing company identity
      change 102–3
    promotion of as a positive for the
      organisation 74–5
    speed of 91–5, 101–2, 228

Chrysler 41–2

Cisco 34, 222

clarity 120
    from CEO 95–7
    organisational redesign 133-4

communication 23, 187–203
    assessment of 201–2
    bad news 137–8
    bidirectional 21, 226
    celebrating victories 121–2
    communications team 47
    consistent 189, 193
    importance of 188–91, 229
    individual concerns 127–8
    integrity in 194
    jobs 133–4
    leader of 190
    line responsibility 190–1
    listening, importance of 199–200
    middle managers, training and
      support 202–3
    new technology 195, 204
    obsessive 190, 191
    open communications strategy
      193–4
    progress updates 193, 196
    reputation building 74
    rumours 192
    senior executives role 203–4
    stakeholders 56–7, 76–8
    storytelling 197–9
    style 120
    surveys 200
    transaction narrative 70–1
    within team 49

communications goal 192

compromise
    non-negotiable elements 37–8,
    85–7, 196
confidential information 88
consultants
    accountability 184–6
    managing the role of 54–5
creating certainty 133
cross-functional sharing 49
culture
    aspects of 72
    assessment of 226
    communication style 120
    compatability 87
    importance of 35
    incompatibility 35–6, 41–3, 175
cultural alignment 175–7
cultural differences 175–8

Daimler-Benz 41–2
Day One
    checklist 99
    background activities 112–16
    example agenda 104–5
    logistics 103–4
    preparation 98–104
    senior management event 106–10
    social event 110–11
    stakeholder meetings 111–12
'deal fever' 52
'deal momentum' 52
Disney 99
Dresden Papier 97
due diligence 50–4, 227
    putting into practice 34

employee engagement 214
    levels 126
expense procedures, post-M&A 115

Facebook 71
Falconbridge 100, 109–10, 172–4
feedback 198–9, 215
Finance Department input 48–9
focusing on the 'me' issues 21, 226
frameworks, to facilitate success of
    M&A 17

Glatfelter 97
Glaxo Wellcome 130
globalisation, effect on M&A 16
goal setting 121

Human Resources 48

impression, creating the right one
    67–80
individual concerns124–7
infrastructure, building 178–6
insulation of production and client
    interaction teams 157–8
integration 15–17, 22, 23–4
    behavioural expectations 108
    design, importance of 227
    director, choice of 44–6
    full integration pitfalls 35–6
    management 29
    mental preparation 79–80
    personal worries 76, 79–80
    planning 29, 31–40,
        benefits of early planning 54
        measurement of plan 213
        see also team: picking the
    A-Team
    post-deal 63
    senior executives visibility to
    employees 203–4
    tailored 35–7
    tradecraft 223

electronic repositories 223
visualisation of integrated
    company 81–3
interaction, style of 72–3
internet, as a means of
    communicating 69
institutionalised approach 222–3
IT department input 48–9

Koc 221
Kottler's change management theory
    78
Kraft 42–3, 122

'ladder of inference' 178
lagging indicators 210
leadership
    behaviours 19–20
    importance of 21
Legal Department input 48–9
lies, detrimental effect of 136–7
listening, importance of 199–200
local knowledge 127–8

management of the board and
    internal executives 57–8
management, interim 115–16
management science 15
management team post-A&M 100,
    107
managers, interim 115
Mannesmann 63–4
measurement of what is to be
    managed 21, 224
measurement of integration process
    206–21
    financial returns 219–20
    metrics to be measured 213–15
    operations post-close 220

strategic positioning 219
mental models 65–7
mergers and acquisitions (M&A)
    failures 15–16
messages, importance of the right 99
metrics 207–20
    defensive behaviours in reaction
    to 215
    operational 212
    ownership 216
    quantification of 215–16
Millennium Pharmaceuticals 87
momentum 119, 121–2, 182, 210
    leverage of 194–6
    loss of 150
    sense of 35
monitoring 180–1, 213–14
'Must-Do' activities list 113–15, 116

negotiation, aggressive 62–3

office
    move 100–1
    refurbishment 101
Omnicom 177
opinion, value of 213
Oracle 222
organisational reviews 130-3, 139-40

PartyGaming 96
planning
    before the deal is closed 31–3,
    37–40, 94
        see also integration:
    planning; due diligence
Publicis 177
pursuing early victories 121–2
PVH 222
Quaker Oats 96

'Red Team Review' approaches 103–4
relationships
    bad 63
    post-deal 62–3
reputation, importance of good one
    64, 73–4
resistance, management of 122–4
restructuring the corporate office
    180–1
retention bonuses 135–6
risks 147–64, 226
    adapting to the environment
    159–64
    clarifying objectives 162
    competitors 151
    confronting and mitigating
    153–64
    external environment risks 151–2
    integration plan risks 149–50
    normal business risks 150–1
    prioritisation 161, 163
    programme management 160
    risk registers, creating 153–5
    types of risk 149

Sapient 177
security arrangements, changing
    113–14
selection 34
shareholders 148
Siemens PLM 82
SmithKline Beecham 130
Snapple 96
staff selection 129
staff retention issues 129–42
    clean break with staff not being
    retained 138–42
stakeholders 56–9
    change management 102–3

communication plan 76–8
Day One meetings 111–12
involvement 57
resetting their relationship 151
steering committee 47
support, creating 58–9
synergies 51–4
    underestimation of 54

Takeda 87
target company, understanding
    39–40
targets, meeting 148
team
    autonomy 171
    central integration team, tenure
    of 182–4
    forging 171
    integration 168–85, 226–7
    maintaining a balance 50
    objectives 171
    picking the A-Team 44–50, 227
    size of 49–50
    structure 48
    team building 169–70, 171–2, 177
        activities 169
    types of team 47
team effort
    importance of 30–1
tension between the team closing
    the deal and team delivering the
    integration 146

uncertainty, detrimental effect of
    93, 95
underperformance 148
    root cause 163
values
    group 174

of new organisation 196–7
visible leadership 21, 224
visualisation of integrated company
    81–3
Vodafone 63–4

Xstrata 86, 100–1, 109–10, 156–7,
    172–4, 180, 198, 222
    driving cultural change at 198–9

Zuckerberg, Mark 71

Urbane
BUSINESS

Urbane Publications is dedicated to
developing author voices and publishing business
titles that challenge, educate and inspire.

From trade business titles to innovative
reference books, our goal is to publish what
YOU want to read.

Find out more at
urbanepublications.com